BRITISH STEAM MILITARY CONNECTIONS:

GREAT WESTERN RAILWAY, SOUTHERN RAILWAY, BRITISH RAILWAYS & WAR DEPARTMENT STEAM LOCOMOTIVES

BRITISH STEAM MILITARY CONNECTIONS:

GREAT WESTERN RAILWAY, SOUTHERN RAILWAY, BRITISH RAILWAYS & WAR DEPARTMENT STEAM LOCOMOTIVES

Keith Langston

PEN & SWORD
TRANSPORT

First published in Great Britain in 2018 by
Pen & Sword Transport
An imprint of
Pen & Sword Books Ltd
47 Church Street
Barnsley
South Yorkshire
S70 2AS

ISBN 978 1 47385 329 4

A CIP catalogue record for this book is
available from the British Library.

Typeset in 11pt Minion by Mac Style Ltd, Bridlington, East Yorkshire
Printed and bound in India by Replika Press Pvt Ltd

Pen & Sword Books Limited incorporates the imprints of Atlas,
Archaeology, Aviation, Discovery, Family History, Fiction, History, Maritime, Military,
Military Classics, Politics, Select, Transport, True Crime, Air World, Frontline Publishing,
Leo Cooper, Remember When, Seaforth Publishing, The Praetorian Press, Wharncliffe Local
History, Wharncliffe Transport, Wharncliffe True Crime and White Owl.

For a complete list of Pen & Sword titles please contact
PEN & SWORD BOOKS LIMITED
47 Church Street, Barnsley, South Yorkshire, S70 2AS, England
E-mail: enquiries@pen-and-sword.co.uk
Website: www.pen-and-sword.co.uk

CONTENTS

ACKNOWLEDGEMENTS

This is a Perceptive Images 2018 © publication exclusively for Pen & Sword Books Ltd.

Additional editorial material and specific images were supplied by my good friends David Anderson and John Chalcraft, whose encouragement and shared railway knowledge was invaluable. A book of this nature could not have been compiled without the co-operation of numerous railway photographers and archivists, some of whom unfortunately are no longer with us, but in this publication their fascinating photographs live on.

Photographic libraries whose images have been used include Author, Mike Bentley Collection, Cresselley Photos, Imperial War Museum, Mike Morant Collection, Royal Air Force, Rail Photoprints.

Keith Langston 2018

Individual photographers whose images have been used include: the author, David Anderson, Rob Bendall, Charles Brown, Mike Buck, Franck Cabrol, John Chalcraft, B.J. Daventry, S.A. Devon, Michael Ely, Tim Felce, David Gibson, J.W. Halifax, Andrew Hastie, Alex Israel, C. Jackson, J.L. Johnson, Dave Jones, Gareth Wyn Jones, Marco Kaiser, Fred Kerr, Len Mills, Mike Morant, Paul Pettitt, Adrian Pingstone, Geoff Plumb, Malcolm Ranieri, Philip Ronan, Royal New Zealand Air Force, Peter Skuce, P.H.F. Tovey, Adam Williams, Mike Young.

Chapter 1

INTRODUCTION

Naming

The naming of steam locomotives in particular, and other railway locomotives and rolling stock in general has been an accepted practice since the very first railway locomotives appeared in 1804.

The practice can fairly be said to be a 'very British tradition'. Numbers were also used to identify individual locomotives, although interestingly the Great Western Railway (GWR) Swindon built 'Broad Gauge' locomotives at first carried only names.

The relevant locomotive classes concerned are of importance in that they represent the amazing engineering achievements of an industry now long gone, which in its time employed literally thousands of people. Accordingly, the names of aircraft and naval vessels are a tribute to the workers who built them, often in the most testing of circumstances. The chosen locomotive names are a tribute to the military personnel and citizens of our country, commonwealth and allies who lost their lives in conflicts.

Locomotive names have been inspired by a wide variety of topics and those connected with the military have figured prominently. This publication highlights steam locomotives given names with a military connection and originally built/ designed by the Great Western Railway (GWR), Southern Railway (SR) or their constituent companies, which then came into British Railways (BR) stock in 1948, and also the relevant BR built locomotives.

The people who chose and bestowed locomotive names obviously thought it significantly important to do so, and as such those names and their origins are worthy of investigation and explanation. We must take into account that choices made so many years ago, may not have obvious rationale when judged using 21st century ideals. The majority of name choice origins highlighted are obvious in having been conferred to mark significant historic events, military groups, prominent personnel, battles and machines of war etc. However, all are interesting and in their individual ways help to provide snapshots of Britain's military and social history.

Preserved Southern Railways built Bulleid 'Battle of Britain' class light pacific BR No 34067 TANGMERE (original SR No 21C167) is seen at Hessay on the East Lancashire Railway in May 2008. Built at Brighton Works and introduced into traffic September 1947 and withdrawn by BR in November 1963. *Fred Kerr*

Preserved BR Standard 'Britannia' class 4-6-2 No 70013 OLIVER CROMWELL is seen at LNWR Heritage Ltd adjacent to the Crewe Heritage Centre whilst receiving attention prior to hauling a series of mainline charter trains during 2015. The locomotive is notable as one of the four steam locomotives which worked the last steam railtour on British Railways (BR) in 1968, before the introduction of a steam ban. OLIVER CROMWELL became part of the National Railway Museum's (NRM) collection immediately after the end of steam on BR. *Keith Langston Collection*

The name plate of GWR 'Castle' class No 5073 originally named CRANBROOK CASTLE and in 1940 renamed for a WWII aircraft. *Keith Langston Collection*

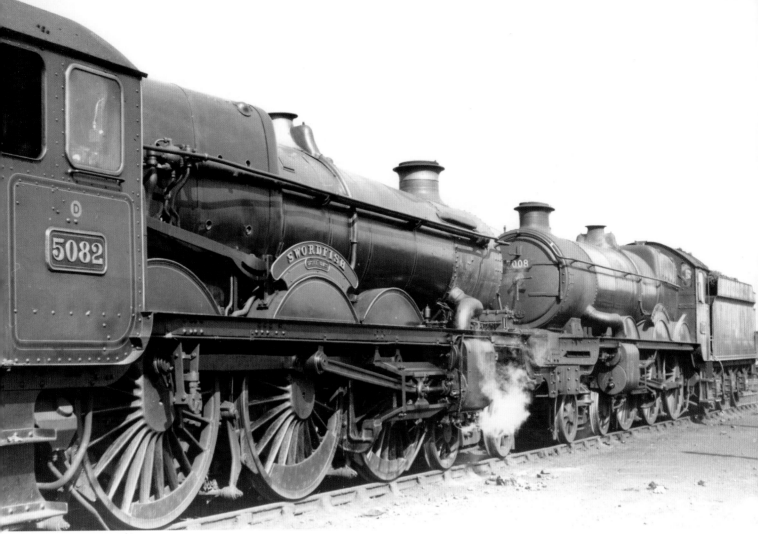

GWR 'Castle' class No 5082 SWORDFISH is seen on shed at Oxford (81F) together with sister engine No 7008 SWANSEA CASTLE in May 1961. Note the additional words CASTLE CLASS on the nameplate of No 5082. *David Anderson*

Locomotives

The GWR 'Castle' class of 4-6-0 locomotives included several which carried military related names, as did the Southern (SR) 'Lord Nelson' class and significantly that company also named a complete class of Light Pacific (4-6-2) locomotives in recognition of the 'Battle of Britain'. Although named after characters in Arthurian Legend relevant locomotives of the 4-6-0 'King Arthur' class are included, as their names can alternatively be linked with contemporary vessels of the Royal Navy. Some locomotives of the SR 'Remembrance', '0458' and '757' classes are also included. A large number of the BR built 'Britannia' Pacific (4-6-2) class were allocated names which can be militarily connected.

To complete the picture a representative selection of 'Austerity' War Department (WD) and Longmoor Military Railway (LMR) steam locomotives with relevant names, is included. There is also a selective listing of preserved Hunslet design 0-6-0 Saddle Tank engines with military connected names, the majority of which were originally supplied to the Ministry of Supply (MOS) as War Department (WD) stock.

Nameplates

As the well-publicized end of the British Railways steam era approached, it became apparent to the naturally observant trackside enthusiasts that nameplates from working locomotives had already started to disappear. Some examples were removed in an excess of a year before the relevant locomotive was withdrawn. In some instances, very poor quality substitutes of a homemade nature were fitted to replace the originals.

If there was an official network, or indeed regional policy, regarding the removal and storage of the nameplates little about it seems to have ever become public knowledge. What is certain however, is that locomotive nameplates have become highly desirable collector's items, not just in the UK but worldwide. There are various railway centres around the UK where steam locomotive nameplates are displayed, some may well be the original article whilst others are reportedly copies, albeit of an accurate nature.

Cast locomotive nameplates have become a big part of the very active trading scene generally described as *Railwayana*, and regular auctions are held. Such events are generally well patronized and the bidding processes create prices which may surprise some readers, not just for items of specific interest but for most genuine nameplates. A recent auction price example, relevant to the locomotives covered herewith include SR 'Lord Nelson' locomotive LORD HOWE which sold in 2016 for £8,500, whilst the relatively small brass crest from the nameplate of GWR 'Castle' class SOUTH WALES BORDERER sold for £10,200. However, auction prices as high as £60,000 for a much sought after steam locomotive nameplate have been recorded.

Cast nameplate which in 2016 realized £8,500 at auction.

Preserved Hunslet 0-6-0ST Austerity WD No198 ROYAL ENGINEER runs around her train at Wootton, on the Isle of Wight Steam Railway 6 October 2013. *Peter Skuce*

Royal Engineers Crest.

Royal Navy Logo.

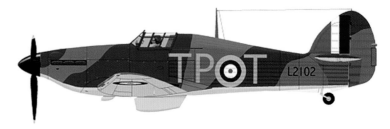

RAF Hawker Hurricane.

Chapter 2

GREAT WESTERN RAILWAY/BRITISH RAILWAYS WESTERN REGION

The Great Western Railway (GWR) group differed from the other three groups in that it was one significant pre-grouping company which then absorbed a further number of smaller Railway Companies during 1922/23. At the time of nationalisation (1948) the total number of steam locomotives owned by the company included engines inherited from no less than 20 previously independent operators.

In January 1948, the majority of the Great Western Railway (GWR) network became British Railways-Western Region (BR/WR). At the end of 1947, the last year of GWR operation, the company's total number of steam locomotives was listed as being 3,856 of which 1,420 were of the tender type and 2429 of the tank locomotive configuration, 7 Narrow Gauge tank engines were also included in the overall total. BR/WR listed all but 77 of those engines in their December 1948 stock of working steam locomotives, and a great many of those carried official names. This publication is for the main part concerned with military connected names carried in both the WWII period and the British Railways (BR) era.

The most important contemporary GWR listing of military associated names is contained in the Collett 'Castle' class 4-6-0 express passenger locomotives, and details of those are included. In addition, other GWR locomotives with historically linked military names are worthy of mention, but are not included in the main listings. In those listings, **P** denotes Preserved Locomotive.

Military Connections – GWR 'Castle' class

In 1948 British Railways inherited some 2,288 locomotives which could be directly attributed to Charles Benjamin Collett O.B.E., almost 60 per cent of the ex-Great Western Railway total. Collett served the Great Western Railway (GWR) for the majority of his working life finally becoming Chief Mechanical Engineer (CME) of that organisation in 1922, a position which he held until his retirement in 1941. Prominent amongst his designs were the highly successful 4-cylinder 4-6-0 'Castle' class locomotives.

The 'Castle' 4073 class represented Collett's first big impact on the GWR and 171 examples were built between 1923 and 1950, all of them at Swindon Works (GWR/BRWR). 'Castle' class engines were coupled to various designs of tender which were regularly interchanged during the locomotives' working lives. A total of 17 'Castle' locomotives were given names with military associations which included 12 named after selected World War II allied aircraft. In most instances named GWR locomotives carried their nameplates over the centre driving wheel splashers.

For full Castle class information see *GWR COLLETT CASTLE CLASS* published by Pen & Sword Books.

GWR Castle 4-6-0 No 111 VISCOUNT CHURCHILL. Originally built in 1908 as GWR Pacific (4-6-2) named **THE GREAT BEAR**, rebuilt as a 'Castle' class engine and put into service in September 1924. Withdrawn in July 1953.

Viscount Churchill. Major Victor Albert Francis Charles Spencer, 1st Viscount Churchill GCVO JP (23 October 1864–3 January 1934), known as The Lord Churchill between 1886 and 1902, was a peer and courtier. Attended Sandhurst and later became a Lieutenant in the Coldstream Guards. He was created the first Viscount Churchill in July 1902 and joined the Great Western Railway Board in 1905; he was elected chairman in 1908 and served longer in that post than anyone else.

The original *GREAT BEAR* name referred to Ursa Major, the star constellation.

Crest of the Coldstream Guards. *J.W. Halifax*

Rebuilt from the GWR Pacific THE GREAT BEAR 'Castle' class 4-6-0 No 111 VISCOUNT CHURCHILL is seen at Plymouth Laira depot (83D), circa 1952. *John Day Collection/Rail Photoprints*

GWR 'Castle' class 4-6-0 No 111 VISCOUNT CHURCHILL is seen at Taunton station with the 6pm service to Penzance on 21 September 1950. *Rail Photoprints Collection*

GWR Castle 4-6-0 No 4016 THE SOMERSET LIGHT INFANTRY (PRINCE ALBERT'S). Originally built as GWR 'Star' class 4-6-0 in April 1908 as No 4016 **KNIGHT OF THE GOLDEN FLEECE.** Rebuilt as a 'Castle' class engine and put into service in October 1925 with its 'Star' class name and number, and subsequently renamed in January 1938. Withdrawn in September 1951.

The Somerset Light Infantry (Prince Albert's) was an infantry regiment of the British Army, which served under various titles from 1685 to 1959. Its lineage is continued today by The Rifles.

The regiment was one of nine regiments of foot raised by James II when he expanded the size of the army in response to the Monmouth Rebellion. The regiment has a long and glorious history and its association with historic wars/ battles includes the Jacobite wars, the American Revolutionary War, French and Napoleonic wars, the Crimean War, The Second Boer War, The First and Second Word wars.

The regiment amalgamated with the Duke of Cornwall's Light Infantry in 1959 to form the Somerset and Cornwall Light Infantry. This, in turn, amalgamated with the three other regiments of the Light Infantry Brigade to form The Light Infantry in 1968.

The final chapter of the Somerset Light Infantry ended on 1 February 2007, when the Devonshire and Dorset Light Infantry, the Light Infantry, the Royal Gloucestershire, Berkshire and Wiltshire Light Infantry and the Royal Green Jackets merged to form the 'Rifles'.

The Regiment's history is exhibited at the Somerset Military Museum, which is a part of the Museum of Somerset at Taunton Castle.

For more information visit www.museumofsomerset.org.uk/somerset-military-museum-3/

Knight of the Golden Fleece: the order of the *Golden Fleece* was established in Burgundy on 10 January 1430 by Philip the Good, Duke of Burgundy and claimed pride of place amongst all Christian orders. It is restricted to a limited number of knights, initially 24 but increased to 30 in 1433, and 50 in 1516, plus the sovereign.

Bronze bust of Allan Francis John Harding, 1st Baron Harding of Petherton who was Colonel of the Somerset Light Infantry 1953–1959. *Keith Langston Collection*

Rebuilt from a 'Star' class locomotive No 4016 KNIGHT OF THE GOLDEN FLEECE is seen at Bristol Bath Road circa 1933. Note the distinctive brass beading on the cab from edges, cab side windows, number/name plates and wheel splashers. *Roy Hinton Collection/Rail Photoprints*

GWR 'Castle' class 4-6-0 No 4016 THE SOMERSET LIGHT INFANTRY (PRINCE ALBERT'S) is seen at Old Oak Common (81A) in April 1950. The locomotive was renamed in a ceremony at Paddington station on 18 February 1938. Note the regimental crest below the nameplate over the centre wheel splasher. *Roy Hinton Collection/Rail Photoprints*

GWR 'Castle' class 4-6-0 No 4037 THE SOUTH WALES BORDERERS is seen approaching Bristol Temple Meads in August 1960. *Rail Photoprints Collection*

GWR Castle 4-6-0 No 4037 THE SOUTH WALES BORDERERS. Originally built as GWR 'Star' class 4-6-0 in December 1910 as No 4037 **QUEEN PHILLIPA**. Rebuilt as a 'Castle' class engine and put into service in June 1926 with its 'Star' class name and number, and subsequently renamed on 14 April 1937. Scrapped December 1962. This member of the class is credited with having the greatest mileage of any GWR engine 2,429,722.

The South Wales Borderers (SWB) was an infantry regiment of the British Army. It first came into existence, as the 24th Regiment of Foot in 1689, but was not called the South Wales Borderers until 1881. The regiment served in a great many conflicts, including the American Revolutionary War, various conflicts in India, the Zulu War, Boer War, and World War I and II.

The SWB was absorbed into the Royal Regiment of Wales in 1969. As its name suggests, it recruited primarily from South Wales. The regimental museum is based at The Barracks, Brecon, South Wales, and claims to have the finest collection of weapons to be found in any regimental museum in the United Kingdom. Its collection of guns shows the development of soldier's weapons from the 18th century to the present.

Drums of the South Wales Borderers. *SWB Museum*

For more information visit www.royalwelsh.org.uk/regimental-museum-of-the-royal-welsh.shtml

Queen Philippa. Philippa of Hainault, married Edward, Prince of Wales, later King Edward III of England. She was married to Edward, first by proxy, when Edward dispatched the Bishop of Coventry 'to marry her in his name' in Valenciennes, Hainaut in October 1327. The marriage was celebrated formally in York Minster on 24 January 1328, some months after Edward's accession to the throne of England. The Queen's College Oxford was founded in her honour. The eldest of her fourteen children was Edward, 'The Black Prince', who became a renowned military leader.

No 4037 QUEEN PHILIPPA is seen as a GWR 'Star' class 4-6-0 circa 1930. *Mike Bentley Collection*

GWR 'Castle' class 4-6-0 No 5017 THE GLOUCESTERSHIRE REGIMENT 28TH 61ST is seen at Cardiff General station having worked in on a service from Gloucester, circa 1957. Note the regimental crest on the centre wheel splasher. *Norman Preedy Collection/Rail Photoprints*

The Gloucestershire Regiment was an infantry regiment of the British Army, and nicknamed 'The Glorious Glosters'. The regiment was formed in Portsmouth in 1694 by Colonel John Gibson and named the 28th Regiment of Foot in 1751, it was renamed the 28th (North Gloucestershire) Regiment of Foot in 1782. On 1st July 1881 the regiment amalgamated with the 61st (South Gloucestershire) Regiment of Foot to form the two-battalion Gloucestershire Regiment. The regiment carried more battle honours on their regimental colours than any other British Army line regiment. Soldiers of the Gloucestershire Regiment and subsequently the Royal Gloucestershire, Berkshire and Wiltshire Regiment wore a cap badge on both the front and the rear of their head dress, a tradition maintained by soldiers in 'The Rifles' when in service dress. The back badge is unique in the British Army and was awarded to the 28th Regiment of Foot for their actions at the Battle of Alexandria in 1801.

'Glosters' regimental colours in Gloucester Cathedral. *Len Mills*

The then Gloucester Horton Road (85B) based GWR 'Castle' class 4-6-0 No 5017 THE GLOUCESTERSHIRE REGIMENT 28TH 61ST heads west out of London near Old Oak Common with a van train, 29 August 1959. *Norman Preedy Collection/Rail Photoprints*

GWR 'Castle' class 4-6-0 No 5017 THE GLOUCESTERSHIRE REGIMENT 28TH 61ST stands at Paddington having worked in with a service from Gloucester, circa 1958. The nameplate and regimental crest were bestowed upon the engine in April, 1954. The renaming was to commemorate the exploits of the 'Glorious Glosters' in general and in particular following their involvement in the Imjin River Battle in Korea. *Crescelley Collection/Rail Photoprints*

Between 1940 and 1941 12 GWR 'Castle' class locomotives were re-named in honour of selected British/Allied World War II aircraft. The choice of names was varied and effectively representative, but to the contemporary reader there are perhaps some notable omissions. Despite its involvement and lasting fame, the world-famous Avro Lancaster bomber was not included whilst the lesser known American built Lockheed Hudson light bomber was. With the benefit of hindsight there were perhaps two other stand out omissions, namely the De-Havilland Mosquito multirole combat aircraft and the Gloster Meteor jet fighter. It is interesting to note that the Meteor jet first flew in 1943 and commenced operations on 27 July 1944 with 616 Squadron RAF.

Loco No	Introduced	Original Name	New name	Withdrawn
5071	July 1938	CLIFFORD CASTLE	**SPITFIRE** – September 1940	October 1963
5072	July 1938	COMPTON CASTLE	**HURRICANE** – November 1940	October 1962
5073	July 1938	CRANBROOK CASTLE	**BLENHEIM** – November 1940	February 1964
5074	July 1938	DENBIGH CASTLE	**HAMPDEN** – January 1941	May 1964
5075	August 1938	DEVIZES CASTLE	**WELLINTON** – October 1940	September 1962
5076	August 1938	DRYSLLWYN CASTLE	**GLADIATOR** – January 1941	September 1964
5077	August 1938	EASTNOR CASTLE	**FAIREY BATTLE** – October 1940	June 1962
5078	May 1939	LAMPHEY CASTLE	**BEAUFORT** – January 1941	November 1962
5079	May 1939	LYDFORD CASTLE	**LYSANDER** – January 1941	May 1960
5080	May 1939	OGMORE CASTLE	**DEFIANT** – January 1941	April 1963 Preserved
5081	June 1939	PENRICE CASTLE	**LOCKHEED HUDSON** – January 1941	October 1963
5082	June 1939	POWIS CASTLE	**SWORDFISH** – January 1941	July 1962

Selected nameplates of 'Castle' locomotives, not named after castles, including those named for WWII aircraft, had the words **Castle Class** appended below the name.

GWR 'Castle' class 4-6-0 No 5071 SPITFIRE. Introduced into service in July 1938 as **CLIFFORD CASTLE** and renamed in September 1940. Scrapped in May 1964.

See also SR 'Battle of Britain' class locomotive No 34066, page 126.

GWR 'Castle' class 4-6-0 No 5071 SPITFIRE approaches Dainton Tunnel with the down 'Cornishman', were you the young spotter standing close to the up track on 26 July 1955? *Norman Preedy Archive/Rail Photoprints*

Spitfire – Supermarine Spitfire, was a British single-seat fighter aircraft designed for the RAF by Reginald Joseph Mitchell CBE, FRAeS. Mitchell continued to refine the design until his death in 1937, whereupon his colleague Joseph Smith took over as chief designer, overseeing the development of the Spitfire through its multitude of variants. The aircraft was used by Great Britain and her allies during and after the Second World War. Powered by the legendary Rolls-Royce Merlin and with a top speed of 370 mph (595 km/h) the Spitfire was perceived by the public to be the main RAF fighter aircraft during the Battle of Britain (July–October 1940). The Spitfire was built with several wing configurations, and was produced in greater numbers than any other British aircraft. It was also the only British

A legendary Spitfire in flight.

fighter to be in continuous production throughout the Second World War. The Spitfire continues to be popular among enthusiasts; about 54 remain airworthy, while many more are static exhibits in aviation museums throughout the world. The number built is generally accepted to be 20,351, aircraft manufactured between 1938 and 1948.

Supermarine Spitfire Mk IIA (Royal Air Force code P7350) at Kemble Air Day, Kemble Airport, Gloucestershire, England, in June 2008. Owned by the UK Battle of Britain Memorial Flight. Quote from the BBMF website: 'P7350 is the oldest airworthy Spitfire in the world and the only Spitfire still flying today to have actually fought in the Battle of Britain. She is believed to be the 14th aircraft of 11,989 built at the Castle Bromwich 'shadow' factory, Birmingham. Entering service in the August of 1940, she flew in the Battle of Britain serving with 266 Squadron and 603 (City of Edinburgh) AuxAF Squadron'. *Adrian Pingstone*

GWR 'Castle' class 4-6-0 No 5071 SPITFIRE approaches Starcross with the down 'Cornishman', 20 September 1954. *Norman Preedy Archive/Rail Photoprints*

'The Cornishman', inaugural titled run 30 June 1952, last titled run 3 May 1975. Originally Wolverhampton Low Level–Penzance, Sheffield Midland–Penzance 10 September 1962, Bradford Foster Square–Penzance 14 June 1965 and Bradford Exchange–Penzance from 1 May 1967.

'Cheltenham Spa Express', inaugural titled run 11 June 1956, last titled run 4 May 1973. Paddington–Cheltenham Spa (St James).

www.youtube.com/watch?v=e33yGl-7uvE
Spitfire Mk1-Dunkirk veteran

The down 'Cheltenham Spa Express' speeding westwards through Sonning Cutting behind GWR 'Castle' class 4-6-0 No 5071 SPITFIRE, during August 1958. *Alan Barkus/Rail Photoprints*

GWR 'Castle' class 4-6-0 No 5072 HURRICANE. Introduced into service in July 1938 as **COMPTON CASTLE** and renamed in November 1940. Scrapped in April 1963.

See also SR 'Battle of Britain' class locomotive No 34065, page 124.

www.youtube.com/watch?v=-EyCvz60R78 Building a 'Castle' class locomotive. *Vintage Trains*

GWR 'Castle' Class 4-6-0 No 5072 HURRICANE is seen outside Chester General station in 1962. Note the words Castle Class appended below the name. *Rail Photoprints Collection*

GWR 'Castle' class 4-6-0 No 5072 HURRICANE is seen passing Tuffley in July 1955. Note the fireman's shovel sticking out above the Hawksworth tender side. *Norman Preedy/Rail Photoprints*

Hurricane – The Hawker Hurricane, designed by Sydney Camm was a British single-seat fighter aircraft used in WWII by Great Britain and her allies, manufactured in several variants. The Hurricane was built by Hawker Aircraft Ltd during the 1930s; it had a maximum speed of 340 mph (547 km/h). During the Battle of Britain, the Hurricanes were recognised by the air force as renowned fighter aircraft which accounted for approximately 60 per cent of the RAF's air victories in the battle. The 1930s-design evolved through several versions and adaptations, resulting in a series of aircraft which acted as fighters, bomber-interceptors, fighter-bombers (also called 'Hurribombers') and ground support aircraft. Further versions known as the Sea Hurricane had modifications which enabled operation from ships. Some were converted as catapult-launched convoy escorts, known as 'Hurricats'. More than 14,583 Hurricanes were built by the end of 1944 (including at least 800 converted to 'Sea Hurricanes and some 1,400 were built in Canada by Canadian Car & Foundry Co.)

www.youtube.com/watch?v=Zqle3_G-Eno
Preserved Hawker Hurricane seen in 2013.

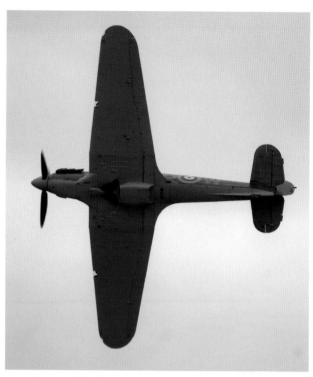

Underside view of 'R4118', a preserved Hurricane from the Battle of Britain. *Adrian Pingstone*

Hawker Hurricane MkIIc of the 'Battle of Britain Memorial Flight', displaying at Kemble Airport Open Day (Gloucestershire, England), on 9 September 2007. This is the last Hurricane ever built, of the 14,533 produced. Built in 1944 and never used in combat. *Adrian Pingstone*

GWR 'Castle' class 4-6-0 No 5073 BLENHEIM. Introduced into service in July 1938 as **CRANBROOK CASTLE** and renamed in January 1941. Scrapped in July 1964.

A fine portrait of ex works GWR 'Castle' class 4-6-0 No 5073 BLENHEIM as it prepares to work a test train at Swindon, 29 June 1950. *Norman Preedy Archive/ Rail Photoprints*

Preserved Duxford Flying Legends, a Bristol Blenheim Mk1 is seen with a Spitfire, on 11 September 2015. *Charlie Jackson*

Blenheim – The Bristol Blenheim was a British light fighter/bomber aircraft designed by Frank Barnwell in 1935. It was built by the Bristol Aeroplane Company and flown by the RAF and allies. The type carried a crew of three airmen, and was one of the first British aircraft to have all-metal stressed-skin, retractable landing gear and flaps, a powered gun turret and variable pitch propellers. The design of the Blenheim proved to be readily adaptable, and was modified to serve in roles such as an interim long-range fighter and as a night fighter.

https://www.youtube.com/watch?v=pS6F0mxVP5E
Bristol Blenheim.

GWR 'Castle' class 4-6-0 No 5074 HAMPDEN. Introduced into service in July 1938 as **DENBIGH CASTLE** and renamed in January 1941. Scrapped in July 1964.

Cardiff Canton depot (86C) allocated GWR 'Castle' class 4-6-0 No 5074 HAMPDEN takes water at Old Oak Common, 12 August 1956. *Norman Preedy Archive/ Rail Photoprints*

Hampden – The Handley Page Hampden 'HP.52' was a Second World War British twin-engine medium bomber used by the RAF and allies. The Hampden was designed by Gustav Lachmann and built by Handley Page Ltd, between 1936–41, in total 1430 of these aircraft were built. Hampdens took part in the first British night raid on Berlin (25 August 1940) and also operated as part of the first 1,000-plane raid on Cologne (30/31 May 1942). The aircraft was nicknamed the 'Flying Suitcase' by aircrews because of the very cramped conditions which the crew members had to endure. The Hampden Mk I had a crew of four: pilot, navigator/bomb aimer, radio operator and rear gunner.

The slim and compact fuselage of the aircraft was quite cramped, wide enough only for a single person. The navigator sat behind the pilot and access in the cockpit required folding down the seats. Once in place, the crew had almost no room to move and was totally uncomfortable during long missions. *Handley Page Archive*

GWR 'Castle' class 4-6-0 No 5074 HAMPDEN is seen arriving at Shrewsbury in the summer of 1956. *Cresselley Archive/ Rail Photoprints*

GWR 'Castle' class 4-6-0 No 5074 HAMPDEN calls at Didcot with the 04.55 Fishguard–Paddington service, circa 1960. Note the schoolboy admirer. *Cresselley Archive/ Rail Photoprints*

GWR 'Castle' class 4-6-0 No 5075 WELLINGTON awaiting entry into Swindon Works, on 17 August 1952 for a Light Intermediate overhaul and tender change. *Norman Preedy Archive/Rail Photoprints*

Wellington – Vickers Wellington long range medium bomber, usually crewed by six persons. These famous WWII bombers were designed by Rex Pierson in the mid-1930s at the aircraft division of Vickers Armstrong, Weybridge, Surrey. In the early years of WWII, the Wellingtons were used on night bombing raids, but they were later replaced on those duties as other four-engine design of heavy bombers became available. In the May 1942 '1000 plus bomber raid' on Cologne, 599 out of the 1,046 total of aircraft were Wellingtons. With Bomber Command, Wellingtons flew some 47,409 operations, during which they dropped an estimated 41,823 tons (37,941 tonnes) of bombs.

Preserved Wellington is seen at RAF Abingdon in 1961.The Wellington was the only British bomber to be produced for the entire duration of the war, and was one of two bombers named after Arthur Wellesley, 1st Duke of Wellington, the other being the Vickers Wellesley. There are two surviving aircraft based in the UK. *David Anderson*

GWR 'Castle' class 4-6-0 No 5076 GLADIATOR introduced into service in August 1938 as **DRYSLLWYN CASTLE** and renamed in January 1941. Scrapped in December 1964.

GWR 'Castle' class 4-6-0 No 5076 GLADIATOR backs down into Paddington station in preparation for working an outbound service, on 30 July 1964. *Chris Davies/Rail Photoprints*

GWR 'Castle' class 4-6-0 No 5076 GLADIATOR leaves Oxford with an Inter-Regional service bound for the Southern Region, in May 1962. *Rail Photoprints Collection*

GWR 'Castle' class 4-6-0 No 5076 GLADIATOR at Shrewsbury shed (84G) in1960, the locomotive carries an 81D Reading (WR) shedplate. Those familiar with the location of this long-closed depot will recall the huge gasholder (aka gasometer) situated nearby. *Norman Preedy Archive/Rail Photoprints*

Gladiator – Gloster Gladiator (also Gloster SS.37) was a British biplane fighter aircraft dating from the 1930s which was designed by Henry Phillip Folland and built by the Gloster Aircraft Company Ltd from 1937 onwards. It was the RAFs last biplane fighter before being rendered obsolete by more modern fighter aircraft. The type, in two variants, which was used by the RAF and allies, also had two naval variants operated by the Fleet Air Arm (FAA). In the early days of WWII, the Gladiators were often sent into combat against more formidable opponents, but nevertheless in the hands of skilled pilots they achieved a fair modicum of success. The biplanes saw action in almost all theatres of the war and notably several of these aircraft took part in the defence of Malta, the George Cross Island.

A stunning image of the preserved Gloster 'Gladiator' K7985. Taken at the Shuttleworth Airshow on 4 July 2010. *Tim Felce*

GWR 'Castle' class 4-6-0 No 5077 FAIREY BATTLE introduced into service in August 1938 as **EASTNOR CASTLE** and renamed in October 1940. Scrapped in August 1962.

GWR 'Castle' class 4-6-0 No 5077 FAIREY BATTLE stands at Newport High Street station with a westbound express, in the summer of 1960. *Norman Preedy Archive/Rail Photoprints*

Fairey Battle – This aircraft was a British single engine light bomber designed by Marcel Lobelle and built from 1936 onwards by the Fairey Aviation Company initially for the RAF, the aircraft had an operating crew of three. The Fairey Battle was powered by the same Rolls-Royce Merlin piston engines which gave other fighter aircraft of that era an edge in combat, however, the advantages of the Merlin engine were somewhat nullified by the Battle's poor power to weight ratio. The aircraft proved to be slow, limited in strike range and extremely vulnerable to both anti-aircraft fire and fighter attacks. By May 1940 the squadrons operating Fairey Battle bombers were reporting a high attrition rate, often in the region of 50 per cent per mission and eventually the Battles were transferred to non-combat duties.

A sergeant air-gunner mans his .303 Vickers 'K-type' gas-operated machine gun from the rear cockpit of a Fairey Battle of No 103 Squadron RAF at St-Lucien Ferme near Rheges. Note the unofficial flight and squadron pennant flying from the radio mast. *S. A Devon RAF*

GWR 'Castle' class 4-6-0 No 5078 BEAUFORT introduced into service in May 1939 as **LAMPHEY CASTLE** and renamed in January 1941. Scrapped in April 1963.

GWR 'Castle' class 4-6-0 No 5078 BEAUFORT is seen at Swindon Station, in 1961. Note the chalked 'Ashes to be cleaned out message' on the smokebox door. *Norman Preedy Archive/Rail Photoprints*

GWR 'Castle' class 4-6-0 No 5078 BEAUFORT is seen at Taunton station on 24 July 1956, with the up 'Devonian'. *David Anderson*

'The Devonian' Bradford Foster Square–Paignton, inaugural run 26 September 1927, Bradford Exchange from 1 May 1967 and Leeds City from 3 May 1971. Last titled run 3 May 1971.

GWR 'Castle' class 4-6-0 No 5078 BEAUFORT enters Paddington station with an up express, on 16 July 1955. Note the early BR logo and also sister engine No 7027 the preserved locomotive THORNBURY CASTLE in the adjacent platform. *C. R. L. Coles (Dave Cobbe Collection) Rail Photoprints*

Beaufort – The Bristol Beaufort was a British twin engine torpedo bomber built by the Bristol Aeroplane Company and others; they were introduced in 1933 and in total 1,121 of these aircraft were built in Britain. Beauforts first saw service with Royal Air Force Coastal Command and then the Royal Navy Fleet Air Arm from 1940. They were used as torpedo bombers, conventional bombers and mine-layers until 1942 when they were removed from front line service and were found alternative use as trainer aircraft until being declared obsolete by the RAF in 1945. Beauforts saw their most extensive use with the Royal Australian Air Force in the Pacific theatre of war, where they were used until the very end of the war. With the exception of six examples delivered from England, 700 additional Beauforts were constructed in Australia under licence. The Australian Beauforts were built at a plant in Fisherman's Bend, Melbourne, Victoria and also at a new factory at Mascot, New South Wales. To speed up the process drawings, jigs and tools and complete parts for six airframes were supplied by Bristol. The bulk of Australian-built Beauforts used locally available materials.

Beaufort first prototype L4441, at a display of new and prototype aircraft, RAF Northolt May 1939. *Charles E Brown*

GWR 'Castle' class 4-6-0 No 5079 LYSANDER introduced into service in May 1939 as **LYDFORD CASTLE** and renamed in November 1940. Scrapped in June 1960.

GWR 'Castle' class No 5079 LYSANDER leaves Teignmouth with an up express, circa 1955. *Alan H. Bryant ARPS/Rail Photoprints*

Lysander – Westland Lysander was a British army co-operation and liaison aircraft designed in 1936 by Arthur Davenport and Teddy Petter and produced by Westland Aircraft, a total of 1,786 were built. These aircraft were used immediately before and during the Second World War by the RAF and allies. After becoming obsolete in the army co-operation role, the aircraft's exceptional short-field performance enabled them to be used on clandestine missions operating to small, unprepared airstrips behind enemy lines to place or recover agents, particularly in occupied France (with the help of the French Resistance). Like other British army air co-operation aircraft, it was given the name of a mythical or legendary leader, in this case that of the Spartan general Lysander. In addition to the RAF, Lysanders were flown by the Indian Air Force, the Royal Canadian Air Force, the Egyptian Air Force and the United States Army Air Force.

During August 1941, a new squadron No 138 (Special Duties) was formed to undertake missions behind enemy lines. Included amongst its allotted aircraft were Lysander Mk IIIs. This airworthy preserved example was seen at RAF Abingdon in 1961. *David Anderson*

GWR 'Castle' class 4-6-0 No 5080 DEFIANT introduced into service in May 1939 as **OGMORE CASTLE** and renamed in January 1941. Locomotive withdrawn May 1962 and preserved.

GWR 'Castle' class 4-6-0 No 5080 DEFIANT spent eleven years in Barry scrapyard before being purchased by the Birmingham Railway Museum Trust and was the 62nd departure from Barry in August 1974. No 5080 returned to the main line during May/June 1988. Thereafter DEFIANT visited numerous heritage railway locations which included the Gloucestershire & Warwickshire, Great Central, Llangollen and the Mid Hants railways. The locomotive was withdrawn from service in 1997 pending an overhaul. It was on static display in 2018 at the Buckinghamshire Railway Centre, Quainton.

Newly restored preserved GWR 'Castle' class 4-6-0 No 5080 DEFIANT with the 'Red Lion' headboard is seen during its triumphant return to mainline steam duties, on Hatton Bank 11 May 1988. The Red Dragon service between London and Carmarthen is known in Welsh as 'Y Ddraig Goch'. *Malcolm Ranieri*

Defiant – The Boulton Paul Defiant was a twin seat British interceptor aircraft that served with the Royal Air Force and allies during the Second World War. The Defiant was designed by John Dudley North and first flew in 1937. It was built by Boulton Paul Aircraft from 1939 onwards and was designated a 'turret fighter', without any forward-firing guns. The plane was powered by the famous Rolls-Royce Merlin V12 engine. The concept of a 'turret fighter' related directly to the successful First World War-era Bristol F.2 Fighter. However, the lack of forward armament proved to be a major weakness in daylight combat and its potential was better realised when it switched to a night combat role. Amongst RAF pilots the type earned the nickname 'Daffy'.

Flight Sergeant E. R. Thorn (pilot, left) and Sergeant F. J. Barker (air gunner) pose with their Boulton Paul Defiant turret fighter at RAF Biggin Hill, Kent after destroying their 13th Axis aircraft. Note the teddy-bear mascot. *P.H.F. Tovey RAF*

GWR 'Castle' class 4-6-0 No 5080 DEFIANT, nameplate pictured during a May 1996 visit to the Llangollen Railway. *Keith Langston Collection*

This preserved locomotive was first allocated to Old Oak Common in 1939 thereafter Cardiff Canton August 1940, Swindon January 1941, Cardiff Canton March 1941, Swindon August 1949, Cardiff Canton September 1949, Landore December 1955 and Llanelly (87F) in September 1961 from where it was withdrawn in May 1962.

GWR 'Castle' class 4-6-0 No 5080 'DEFIANT' sits on the ash pit at Old Oak Common (81A), during 1959. *Norman Preedy Archive/Rail Photoprints*

Preserved GWR 'Castle' class 4-6-0 No 5080 DEFIANT seen whilst crossing the picturesque Berwyn Viaduct on scenic Llangollen Railway in North Wales. In addition to hauling service trains, during a May 1996 visit, the locomotive was used on several 'Driver Experience Trains', this is one such run. Note the locomotive carries GWR livery, and also has its number stencilled on the front buffer beam. A TYS Tyseley shed marking on the side plating over the bogie and also BR overhead power cable warning stickers, no doubt a hangover from the engine's mainline charter days. *Keith Langston Collection*

GWR 'Castle' class 4-6-0 No 5080 DEFIANT seen 'on shed' at the Llangollen Railway. *Keith Langston Collection*

https://www.youtube.com/watch?v=TbHItCgomLM
GWR 'Castle' No 5080 DEFIANT, on Llanvihangel bank in 1988.

To commemorate the Coronation of HRH Queen Elizabeth II in 1953 certain named trains carried celebratory headboards. On 23 May 1953 at Paddington station GWR 'Castle' class 4-6-0 No 5081 LOCKHEED HUDSON carried a 'Bristolian' headboard while alongside an unidentified GWR 'King' class 4-6-0 displays an 'Inter City' headboard. *Ray Hinton Collection/Rail Photoprints*

'The Bristolian' Paddington–Bristol Temple Meads inaugural run 9 September 1935, title withdrawn 9 September 1939. Reintroduced 2 July 1951, last titled run 12 June 1965. 'Inter City' Paddington–Wolverhampton Low Level inaugural run 25 September 1950, last titled run 12 June 1965.

Lockheed Hudson – The Lockheed Hudson was perhaps an unusual choice to be included in the 'Castle' class aircraft of WWII listings, particularly when the famous British built Lancaster bomber and the American built Flying Fortress (B17) were both omitted. The Lockheed Hudson was an American light bomber and coastal patrol twin engined aircraft designed by Clarence 'Kelly' Johnson and a total of 2,941 were built in several variants between 1938–43 by the Lockheed Aircraft Corporation, for the RAF and allies. The Hudson served throughout WWII, mainly with Coastal Command but also in transport and training roles as well as delivering agents by parachute into occupied France. They were also used extensively with the Royal Canadian Air Force's anti-submarine squadrons and by the Royal Australian Air Force.

A preserved Lockheed Hudson Patrol Bomber of the Royal New Zealand Air Force, painted in the colours of an aircraft of No 4 Squadron RNZAF (circa 1942–1944). Photographed at the RNZAF Museum, Wigram NZ. *RNZAF Museum*

GWR 'Castle' class 4-6-0 No 5082 SWORDFISH introduced into service in June 1939 as POWIS CASTLE and renamed in January 1941. Scrapped December 1962.

GWR 'Castle' class 4-6-0 No 5082 SWORDFISH is seen approaching Exeter (St. David's) with the 12 noon Penzance-Crewe 'mails' on 30 July 1956. Note the on the move mailbag exchange equipment attached to the leading mail coach. *David Anderson*

Swordfish – The Fairey Swordfish was a torpedo bomber biplane designed by the Fairey Aviation Company and a total of 2,391 were built between 1936–44. They were used by the Fleet Air Arm of the Royal Navy during the Second World War. Originating in the 1930s, the Swordfish, nicknamed 'Stringbag' by the aircrews, was an outdated design by the start of the war in 1939, but remarkably continued to fly in front-line combat service until VE Day (8 May 1945 – Victory in Europe). The Swordfish achieved some spectacular successes, notably the sinking of one and damaging of two other battleships of the Italian Navy in the Battle of Taranto (11–12 November 1940), and also the crippling of the famous German battleship Bismarck (26–27 May 1941).

Three Fairey Swordfish Mark IIIs of No. 119 Squadron RAF, seen flying in loose starboard echelon formation over the North Sea during WWII. *B.J. Daventry (Flt Lt), RAF*

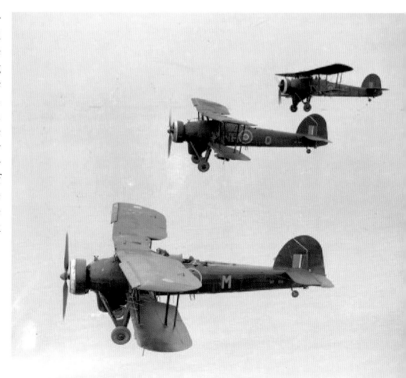

In the period 1885 to 1971 two individuals carried similar Viscount Portal titles. The first being *Wyndham Raymond Portal 1st Viscount Portal PC, GCMG, DSO, MVO* (1885–1949). Being the last chairman of the Great Western Railway it was this gentleman for whom 'Castle' class engine No 7000 was named.

He was commissioned into the Hampshire Yeomanry in 1903, promoted Lieutenant in 1905, and transferred to the 9th Lancers later the same year. Joining the 1st Life Guards as a Second Lieutenant in 1908 he was again promoted to Lieutenant, but left the Army in 1911. He rejoined the Hampshire Yeomanry in 1914 and served in World War I. He was promoted Captain in 1914 while serving as adjutant of the Royal 1st Devon Yeomanry. Transferring back to the Life Guards (Special Reserve) in 1915, he was promoted Lieutenant-Colonel in 1916 taking command of the Household Battalion. In 1917 he was awarded the Distinguished Service Order (DSO) and appointed a Member of the Royal Victorian Order (MVO). He relinquished command of the battalion in 1918 and in that year reverted to the rank of Captain. He was promoted Major and later Lieutenant-Colonel with the Machine Gun Corps as battalion commander. He resigned his commission in 1919.

However, also worthy of mention is Charles Portal, 1st Viscount Portal of Hungerford who had a distinguished career with the RAF.

Charles Frederick Algernon Portal, 1st Viscount Portal of Hungerford, KG, GCB, OM, DSO & Bar, MC, DL (1893–1971). In the First World War Portal was a pilot, a flight commander and a squadron commander who flew light bombers on the Western Front. At the beginning of WWII, he was commander-in-chief of Bomber Command. It was he who advocated strategic area bombing against German industrial areas. Later becoming Chief of the Air Staff he fended off an attempt by the Royal Navy to take over RAF Coastal Command and in addition, an attempt by the British Army to establish their own Army Air Arm. In retirement Portal was chairman of British Aluminium and then chairman of the British Aircraft Corporation (BAC).

The 9 February 1945 Yalta Conference. Seated: Winston Churchill, Franklin D. Roosevelt and Josef Stalin. Standing: Admiral of the Fleet Sir Andrew Cunningham, RN, Marshal of the Royal Air Force Sir Charles Portal RAF and Fleet Admiral William D. Leahy, USN and Soviet officers. *U.S. Signal Corps*

Machine Gun Corps Memorial, Hyde Park Corner, London. *Mike Young*

GWR 'Castle' class 4-6-0 No 7000 VISCOUNT PORTAL is seen at Exeter St. David's during July 1955 with an up 'Devonian' working. *David Anderson*

GWR 'Castle' class 4-6-0 No 7000 VISCOUNT PORTAL is seen entering Newton Abbott station with the up 'Torbay Express' during the summer of 1959. *Rail Photoprints Collection*

A selection of Additional GWR locomotives with military names

GWR Churchward 'Saint' class 4-6-0 No 2980 (scrapped August 1951) was named COEUR DE LION, and that name was also carried by BR Standard 'Britannia' class locomotive No 70007 COEUR-DE-LION, see page 187.

Several GWR Churchward 'Star' class 4-6-0 locomotives, which came into BR stock (1948) were named for 'Orders of Knights', several members of which had military connections.

4012	KNIGHT OF THE THISTLE	Scrapped December 1949
4013	KNIGHT OF ST. PATRICK	Scrapped June 1950
4015	KNIGHT OF ST. JOHN	Scrapped April 1951
4017	KNIGHT OF LIEGE	Scrapped January 1950
4018	KNIGHT OF THE GRAND CROSS	Scrapped December 1949
4019	KNIGHT TEMPLAR	Scrapped April 1951
4020	KNIGHT COMMANDER	Scrapped October 1952

GWR 'Star' class 4-6-0 No 4017 KNIGHT OF LIEGE is seen circa 1929. This Swindon built locomotive was introduced into service during 1908 as KNIGHT OF THE BLACK EAGLE and renamed in 1914. *Rail Photoprints Collection*

GWR 'Star' class 4-6-0 No 4018 KNIGHT OF THE GRAND CROSS, awaiting the cutters torch at Swindon, on 19 June 1951. *Rail Photoprints Collection*

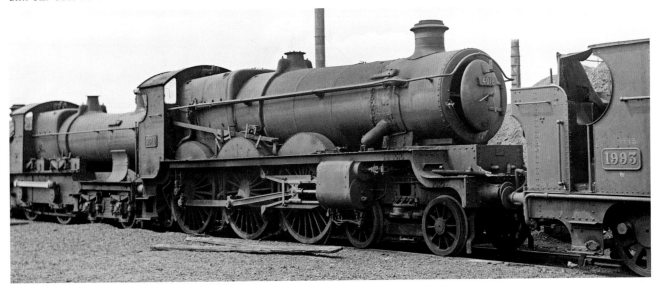

GWR 'Star' class 4-6-0 No 4019 KNIGHT TEMPLAR seen above at Old Oak Common in 1920 and below again at Old Oak Common in 1935. *Both images Rail Photoprints Collection*

Insignia Knight of the Thistle

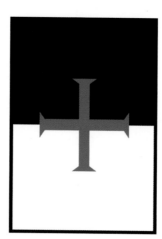

Knight Templar Flag

Insignia Knight of St. Patrick

Vale of Rheidol Railway

Vale of Rheidol (VoR) preserved narrow gauge 2-6-2T locomotive No 7, which was a British Railways engine between 1948 and 1989 is named for the Welsh warrior and hero OWAIN GLYNDWR. That name, although originally spelt differently, was also carried by the BR Standard 'Britannia' class locomotive No 70010 OWEN GLENDOWER, see page 190.

Vale of Rheidol (VoR) preserved narrow gauge 2-6-2T locomotive No 7 OWAIN GLYNDWR is seen waiting to depart from Aberystwyth station with a train for Devils Bridge in the mid-1960s. Note the BR blue livery complete with inter-city logo. *David Anderson*

Vale of Rheidol (VoR) preserved narrow gauge 2-6-2T locomotive No 7 OWAIN GLYNDWR in BR/WR green livery is seen outside the locomotive shed at Aberystwyth. *John Chalcraft/Rail Photoprints*

The Vale of Rheidol Light Railway was authorised by Act of Parliament on 6th August 1897. At the time of building, it was of the most up to date standard of narrow gauge construction, and passed through terrain where it would have been almost impossible to build a standard gauge line without prohibitive costs.

For more information visit http://www.rheidolrailway.co.uk/

Arriving, VoL locomotive No 7 OWAIN GLYNDWR is seen in mottled light whilst approaching Devils Bridge station.

Arrived, VoL locomotive No 7 OWAIN GLYNDWR in Devils Bridge station. Both images taken in May 1995. *Keith Langston Collection*

Chapter 3

SOUTHERN RAILWAY/BRITISH RAILWAYS SOUTHERN REGION

The Southern Railway (SR) was formed in 1923 by the amalgamation of three major railway companies which were themselves formed by the acquisition and merger of several smaller railway companies. In January 1948 the majority of the Southern Railway network became British Railways-Southern Region.

At the end of 1947, the last year of Southern Railway operation, the company's total number of steam locomotives was listed as being 1,851 of which 1,151 were of the tender type and 693 of the tank locomotive configuration, a further 7 tank engines were listed as Service Locomotives. BR/SR listed all but 60 of those engines in their 1948 stock of working steam locomotives and a total of 329 of those carried official names. In addition, there were a number of ex London, Brighton & South Coast Railway (LBSCR) and South Eastern & Chatham Railway – Southern Railway, (SECR/SR) BR/SR locomotives which carried names for a period under former ownership, but not as BR locomotives. A large number SR locomotive names had a direct connection with the 'military' whilst others had a historic and/or secondary connection. As previously stated this publication is for the main part concerned with military connected names carried in British Railways (BR) ownership. In the listings **P** denotes Preserved Locomotive.

The Southern Railway network was by the very nature of its geographical location on the 'front line' during both World Wars and was particularly vulnerable during the World War II Battle of Britain, the bombing Blitz and the threatened invasion by German forces. The coastal areas it served were crucial to the Allies during the movement of troops and war materials to and from the occupied territories and theatres of war. A large proportion of Britain's naval fleet and many military airfields and army camps were based in the region. The railways in general, and the SR in particular, played a crucial part in supporting those defending the British nation. Therefore, it is not surprising that, with government approval the Southern Railway authorities decided to name a whole class of steam locomotives in remembrance of the Battle of Britain. In addition, other BR/SR steam locomotives proudly carried names linked with the military.

Preserved 'Battle of Britain' class Bulleid Light Pacific locomotive BR No 34070 MANSTON makes a fine sight when seen hard at work on the Swanage Railway during October 2010. *David Gibson*

'Battle of Britain' class Bulleid Light Pacific locomotive BR No 34086 219 SQUADRON is pictured exiting the western portal of Honiton Tunnel with a London Waterloo–Exeter–Plymouth express service on 26 July 1956. The photographer noted that this was a very hot summers day, with the mid-day temperature reaching 85 degrees Fahrenheit!
David Anderson

'L' class Baltic Tank (4-6-4) SR No 2333 REMEMBRANCE is seen at New Cross Gate in 1928. This locomotive was built at Brighton Works and entered service in April 1922 as LBSCR No 333, it was the last new locomotive built by the London, Brighton and South Coast Railway. Note the side footstep brackets, tank end panel footsteps and handrail in order to allow access to the water tank filler door situated on top of the tank. *Rail Photoprints Collection*

The Southern Railway/British Railways 'N15X Remembrance' class locomotives were originally built as 4-6-4 (Baltic) tank engines by the LBSCR between 1914 and 1922 to an L. B. Billinton design, designated 'L' class. Seven of the Baltic Tanks were built and were mainly intended for use as express passenger locomotives on the Brighton and Eastbourne routes, all of them were named. Six of the class carried the names of famous locomotive engineers; however, the seventh (like the class) was named REMEMBRANCE in memory of the men of the LBSCR who lost their lives in the First World War. Between 1934 and 1936 the class of tank locomotives were replaced by electric trains on the aforementioned routes and the Southern then decided to rebuild them as 4-6-0 tender locomotives to an R.E.L. Maunsell design, which incorporated 8-wheel tenders. In 1948 the 'N15X' class was taken into BR stock and allocated the number series 32327–32333. The 'N15X' class spent their careers at Basingstoke depot (70D) and were mainly used on secondary duties.

Billinton

Lawson Butzkopfski (or Boskovsky) Billinton (1882–1954) was the Locomotive Engineer of the London, Brighton and South Coast Railway (LBSCR) from 1912 until 1923. He joined the LBSCR in 1900 as an apprentice and in 1907 became a district locomotive superintendent at New Cross. In 1911, due to the absence through ill health of the railway's Chief Engineer D.E. Marsh he became caretaker Chief Engineer at Brighton works, being promoted to Locomotive Engineer at the beginning of 1912 after Marsh retired. In 1917 Billinton was commissioned as a temporary Lieutenant Colonel in the Royal Engineers, and he served on military missions to Romania and Russia. He retired from the SR aged 40 in 1923, taking up fruit farming in Sussex. Billinton died in 1954 at Lyme Regis, Dorset.

SR 'N15X' class SR No 2333 REMEMBRANCE (later BR No 32333) is seen ex works at Eastleigh in 1934. *Rail Photoprints Collection*

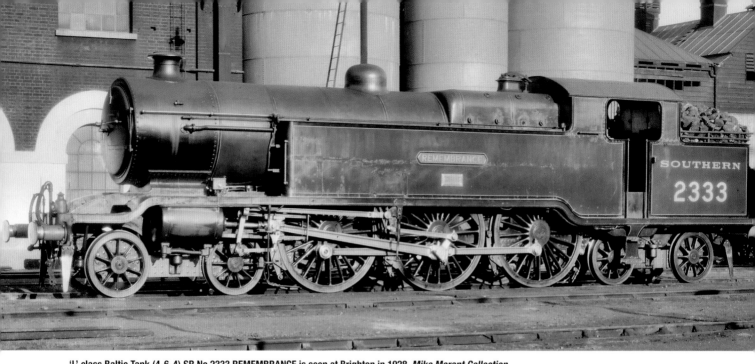

'L' class Baltic Tank (4-6-4) SR No 2333 REMEMBRANCE is seen at Brighton in 1928. *Mike Morant Collection*

SR 'N15X' class BR No 32333 REMEMBRANCE is pictured also at Brighton depot (then 75A). The date is uncertain but must be during, or after 1952 (note the BR Standard 'Class4 Tank' beyond the tender of the 4-6-0). The engine's motion, cylinder covers, nameplate, firebox plugs and buffers and hook are embellished (although white painted not traditionally burnished) presumably for some special event but the locomotive is generally in need of a clean! *Mike Morant Collection*

Class Details

'L' Class 4P	4-6-4T	7 built 1914/22 Brighton	Driving Wheel 6ft 9ins dia	2- outside cylinders Walschaert piston valves	Working BP 180psi Superheated Tractive effort 23325lbf
'N15X' Class 4P	4-6-0	7 re-built 1934/36 Brighton	Driving Wheel 6ft 9ins dia	2- outside cylinders Walschaert piston valves	Working BP 180psi Superheated Tractive effort 23325lbf

Preserved SR Maunsell 'Lord Nelson' (LN) class 4-6-0 is seen as SR No 850 LORD NELSON. Built in 1926 this locomotive was retired by BR in August 1962 and it is now part of the National Collection. In preservation, this 'LN' locomotive has frequently operated on the national network and also visited several heritage railways. *Keith Langston Collection*

Southern Railway 'LN' Lord Nelson class 4-6-0

The SR class 'LN' or Lord Nelson class is a type of 4-cylinder 4-6-0 steam locomotive designed for the Southern Railway by Richard Maunsell, built at Eastleigh Works they were introduced between 1926 and 1929. The 'Lord Nelson' class locomotives were originally designed to haul the numerous Continental boat trains between London (Victoria) and Dover (Harbour), but were also later used for general express passenger work between the capital and the South-West of England. Sixteen of them were constructed and at the time they were the most powerful SR 4-6-0 locomotives. They were all named after famous admirals. British Railways took into stock all 16 of the class and began scrapping them in 1961. The class leader, SR No 850 (BR 30850) LORD NELSON is the only member of the class which survived into preservation and it is a part of the National Collection.

Maunsell

Irish born locomotive engineer Richard Edward Lloyd Maunsell (1868–1944) attended Trinity College Dublin and in 1888 joined the Gt. South Western Railway (Gt.SWR) at Inchicore Works Dublin. He moved to the Lancashire & Yorkshire Railway, Horwich in 1891 before, in 1894, joining the East Indian Railway in Bengal. In 1896 Maunsell returned to the Gt.SWR taking up the post of Inchicore Works Manager. He remained with the Gt.SWR until 1913, having been promoted to the post of Chief Mechanical Engineer (CME) in 1911. Moving to England in 1913 he became CME of the South Eastern and Chatham Railway (SECR) a company which in 1923 became the Southern Railway (SR). He retired in October 1937 and died at Ashford, Kent on 7 March 1944.

The 'LN' class nameplates were carried on the splasher over the centre driving wheel. Interestingly the nameplate of No 30850 LORD NELSON was the only one of the class which did not carry the additional words LORD NELSON CLASS shown under the name.

30850 LORD NELSON (SR No 850) entered SR service 8/1926, coupled with a 5000 gallon/5 ton tender. Withdrawn from BR service August 1962, this locomotive is part of the National Collection (NRM). In 2018 the locomotive was based at the Mid-Hants Railway and reported as being operational. **P**

Horatio Nelson, 1st Viscount Nelson, KB born Burnham Thorpe, Norfolk, (29 September 1758–21 October 1805) was a British flag officer in the Royal Navy. He was greatly revered for his inspirational leadership and superb grasp of naval strategy. He was wounded several times in combat, losing one arm in the unsuccessful attempt to conquer Santa Cruz de Tenerife and the sight of one eye during action off Corsica. Nelson was shot and killed during his fleet's final victory at the Battle of Trafalgar in 1805, whilst aboard his flag ship HMS *Victory*. The battle was the most decisive naval victory of the war in which 27 British ships of the line defeated 33 French and Spanish ships of the line, commanded by French Admiral Pierre-Charles Villeneuve. The battle took place in the Atlantic off the southwest coast of Spain, west of Cape Trafalgar. The Franco-Spanish fleet lost twenty-two ships, but not a single British vessel was lost. Admiral Lord Nelson's body was brought back to England where he was accorded a state funeral. His most famous, and frequently quoted signal was 'England expects that every man will do his duty'. HMS *Victory* can be visited at the Historic Dockyard, Portsmouth.
See also http://www.hms-victory.com/

The famous Nelson's column in Trafalgar Square, London. *Keith Langston Collection*

Preserved SR Maunsell 'Lord Nelson' (LN) class 4-6-0 No 850 LORD NELSON is seen at Hellifield in 1985, preparing to join its train during 'Cumbrian Mountain Express' duty (CME). *Keith Langston Collection*

Maunsell 'Lord Nelson' (LN) class 4-6-0 BR No 30850 LORD NELSON is seen beneath the impressive array of signals at Bournemouth station during June 1954. Note the early BR crest. *Rail Photoprints Collection*

Maunsell 'Lord Nelson' (LN) class 4-6-0 BR No 30850 LORD NELSON is seen passing Didcott with the return leg of a 'Home Counties Railway Club Special', June 1962. *David Anderson*

https://www.youtube.com/watch?v=Pl0Da-G4vR8
No 850 in Steam! Lord Nelson at the East Lancashire Railway.

30851 SIR FRANCIS DRAKE (SR No 851) entered SR service June 1928 coupled with a 5000 gallon/5 ton tender. Withdrawn from BR service December 1961, cut up May 1962.

Arms of Sir Francis Drake; Sable, a fess wavy between two pole-stars Arctic and Antarctic argent.

Sir Francis Drake, Vice Admiral born Tavistock, Devon (c.1540–27 January 1596) was an Elizabethan sea captain, privateer, navigator, slaver, and politician. Drake carried out the second circumnavigation of the world in a single expedition, from 1577 to 1580 and the vessel concerned was the Pelican (later renamed Golden Hind). Queen Elizabeth I awarded Drake a knighthood in 1581. He was second in command of the English fleet that famously did battle with the Spanish Armada in 1588. He died of dysentery in January 1596 after unsuccessfully attacking San Juan, Puerto Rico. He was a great hero to the English; however, King Philip II of Spain considered him to be a pirate (and accordingly nicknamed him *El Draque – The Dragon*) the Spanish ruler reportedly offered a reward of 20,000 ducats (about £4 million by modern standards) for Drake's life. A popular cocktail of the era named *El Draque* (modern times Mojito) is attributed to Drake.

30852 SIR WALTER RALEIGH (SR No 852) entered SR service July 1928 coupled with a 5000 gallon/5 ton tender. Withdrawn from BR service February 1962, cut up March 1962.

Sir Walter Raleigh born East Budleigh, Devon (c.1554–29 October 1618) was an English gentleman, writer, poet, soldier, politician, courtier, spy, and explorer and cousin to Sir Richard Grenville and younger half-brother of Sir Humphrey Gilbert. He is perhaps mainly remembered for popularizing tobacco in England. He rose rapidly to favour with Queen Elizabeth I who bestowed a knighthood on him in 1585. In what could be rightly described as an eventful life Raleigh was twice imprisoned in the Tower of London, firstly for marrying, without permission, one of the Queen's ladies in waiting and secondly for his part in a plot against King James I. After his release, he led an expedition in search of the so called El Dorado during which he took part in an unsuccessful military action against a Spanish outpost in South America. On his return to England (1618), and despite his previous good deeds on behalf of the nation, he was arrested and executed apparently in order to appease the Spanish.

Raleigh statue at the Raleigh Convention Centre North Carolina USA. *Alex Israel*

30853 SIR RICHARD GRENVILLE (SR No 853) entered SR service September 1928 coupled with a 5000 gallon/5 ton tender. Withdrawn from BR service March 1962, cut up April 1962.

Sir Richard Grenville (15 June 1542–10 September 1591) Lord of the manors of Stowe, Kilkhampton in Cornwall and of Bideford in Devon. Grenville was appointed Vice-Admiral of the Fleet under Thomas Howard. He took part in the early English attempts to settle the New World, and also participated in the fight against the Spanish Armada. He was charged with maintaining a squadron at the Azores to waylay the return to Spain of the South American Spanish treasure fleets. He took command of *Revenge*, a galleon considered to be a masterpiece of naval construction. Whilst captain of the *Revenge* he died at the Battle of Flores (1591), fighting heroically against overwhelming odds, and refusing to surrender his ship to the far more numerous Spanish. He was also a soldier, an armed merchant fleet owner, privateer, colonizer, and explorer.

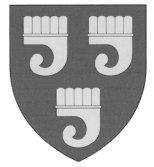

Arms of Grenville of Bideford, Devon and Stowe, Kilkhampton, Cornwall, 3 clarions.

30854 HOWARD OF EFFINGHAM (SR No 854) entered SR service October 1928 coupled with a 5000 gallon/5 ton tender. Withdrawn from BR service September 1961, cut up October 1961.

William Howard, 1st Baron Howard of Effingham (c. 1510–12 January 1573). Admiral Charles Howard was the eldest son of Thomas Howard, 2nd Duke of Norfolk by his second wife, Agnes Tilney. Howard served four monarchs, Henry VIII, Edward VI, Queen Mary and Queen Elizabeth, in various official capacities, including Lord Admiral and Lord Chamberlain of the Household. In 1541 Lord Howard was charged with concealing the sexual indiscretions of his young niece, Katherine Howard, Henry VIII's fifth Queen, and ordered to stand trial. On 22 December 1541 Lord Howard, his wife, and a number of servants who had been alleged witnesses to the Queen's misconduct were convicted, and sentenced to life imprisonment and loss of goods. However, Howard and most of the others were pardoned after Queen Katherine's execution on 13 February 1542. Additionally, Admiral Howard was a patron of the theatre in 1576 a company of actors originally known as *Lord Howard's Men* was formed (later referred to as *The Admiral's Men*) and they are allegedly linked to the first performances of Shakespeare's 'Richard III'.

'Lord Nelson' (LN) class 4-6-0No 30854 HOWARD OF EFFINGHAM, then an Eastleigh (71A) allocated engine, is seen on shed at Nine Elms (70A). *Mike Morant Collection*

30855 ROBERT BLAKE (SR No 855) entered SR service November 1928 coupled with a 5000 gallon/5 ton tender. Withdrawn from BR service September 1961, cut up February 1962.

Robert Blake born Bridgwater, Somerset (27 September 1598–7 August 1657) was reputed to have been one of the most important military commanders of the so-called Commonwealth of England. He was one of the most famous English admirals of the 17th century, whose successes have according to one biographer 'never been excelled, not even by Nelson'. Blake is often regarded as the chief founder of England's legendary naval supremacy, that dominance was continued in the 19th and 20th century by the Royal Navy. In the opinion of some historians the deliberate attempts to expunge many of the 'Parliamentarians' from history following the Restoration (1660) meant that Blake's achievements tended not to receive the full recognition which some consider they deserve.

Arms of Robert Blake: argent, a chevron between three garbs sable.

30856 LORD St. VINCENT (SR No 856) entered SR service November 1928 coupled with a 5000 gallon/5 ton tender. Withdrawn from BR service September 1962, cut up November 1962.

John Jervis, 1st Earl of St. Vincent GCB, PC Admiral of the Fleet, born Stone, Staffordshire (9 January 1735–14 March 1823) was an admiral in the Royal Navy and Member of Parliament in the United Kingdom. Jervis served throughout the latter half of the 18th century and into the 19th, and was an active commander during the Seven Years' War, American War of Independence, French Revolutionary War and the Napoleonic wars. Admiral Sir John Jervis is best known for his triumph at the Battle of Cape Saint Vincent on 14 February 1797, from which he later earned his titles. The battle, between the British and Spanish fleets, took place off the west coast of Portugal, to the north west of the Spanish naval port of Cadiz. Commanding the Spanish fleet was Admiral Don Jose de Cordova. During the battle the British fleet successfully captured two Spanish '3 deckers' and severely damaged several other vessels. Interestingly Jervis's plan, the forerunner of Nelson's aggressive attack at Trafalgar, was to take his fleet in 'line ahead' through the Spanish formation, thus effectively cutting the Spanish Fleet in two.

'Lord Nelson' (LN) class 4-6-0 No 30856 LORD St. VINCENT is seen in light steam at its then home shed Eastleigh (71A) in June 1962, barely 6 months before it was scrapped. *Rail Photoprints Collection*

'Lord Nelson' (LN) class 4-6-0 No 30857 LORD HOWE is seen approaching Eastleigh with an up boat-train in August 1962. Note the then customary baggage car at the head of the train. *Rail Photoprints Collection*

30857 LORD HOWE (SR No 857) entered SR service December 1928 coupled with a 5000 gallon/5 ton tender. Withdrawn from BR service September 1962, cut up October 1962.

Richard Howe, 1st Earl Howe, KG (8 March 1726–5 August 1799) Admiral of the Fleet, was notable for his service during the American War of Independence and French revolutionary wars. Howe served throughout the war of the Austrian Succession having joined the navy at the age of thirteen. During the 'Seven Years War' he gained a reputation for his role in amphibious operations against the French coast. He took part in the decisive British naval victory at the Battle of Quiberon Bay in 1759. He is perhaps best known for his service during the American War of Independence, when he acted as a naval commander and a peace commissioner with the American rebels. He also commanded the British fleet during the mid-Atlantic battle and blockade against the French in 1794, referred to as the 'Glorious First of June'. Remarkably Howe was then 68 years old.

30858 LORD DUNCAN (SR No 858) entered SR service January 1929, coupled with a 5000 gallon/5 ton tender. Withdrawn from BR service August 1961, cut up November 1961.

Admiral Lord Viscount Duncan of Camperdown was born in Dundee (1 July 1731–4 August 1804). Duncan's naval career spanned some 54 years. He saw early service in the search, off the west coast of Scotland, for Prince Charles Edward Stuart (also known as Bonnie Prince Charlie and The Young Pretender) Thereafter he served with distinction in the Royal Navy respectively in the Mediterranean, America, West Africa and Cuba. In his later years, he earned wide respect for his handling of the serious naval mutinies of 1797. Duncan achieved his greatest fame through his remarkable defeat of the Dutch Fleet under the command of Admiral de Winter, off Camperdown (Kamperduin), on 11 October 1797. Duncan's fleet consisted of 24 ships and the Dutch fleet 25 vessels. The victory thwarted a possible invasion of Britain by combined French and Dutch troops. For his various exploits, Duncan was created Baron of Lundie and also given the title Viscount Camperdown.

The statue of Admiral Lord Viscount Duncan, in Dundee. *Keith Langston Collection*

Samuel Hood, 1st Viscount Hood was born in Butleigh, Somerset (12 December 1724–27 January 1816). Admiral Hood is remembered particularly for his service in both the American Revolutionary War and the French Revolutionary Wars. Reportedly he was active in the role of mentor to Horatio Nelson. He lived long enough to see the Seventh Coalition triumph in the Napoleonic Wars and was chief mourner at Nelson's funeral. In addition to his naval activities he was elected as Tory member of Parliament for Westminster for two terms, 1784 to 1788 and 1790 to 1796, and was also member for Reigate between 1789 and 1790, serving under William Pitt the Younger. Two of the three ships of the Royal Navy named HMS *Hood* were named after him, including the HMS *Hood* which was sunk by the *Bismarck* in 1941 during World War II. The admiral is the namesake of Port Hood, Nova Scotia.

'Lord Nelson' (LN) class 4-6-0 BR No 30859 LORD HOOD is seen at Oxford depot (81F). The SR loco has been turned and serviced (including a very full tender of coal) before heading a train back to Bournemouth. Interestingly the ex GWR turntable at Oxford was 'tight' for the visiting 'LN' class engines which had a total length (with tender) of 69 foot 9¾ inches, compared with the GWR 'Castle' class engines at 65ft 3ins. *David Anderson*

30860 LORD HAWKE (SR No 860) entered SR service April 1929, coupled with a 5000 gallon/5 ton tender. Withdrawn from BR service August 1962, cut up August 1962.

Edward Hawke, 1st Baron Hawke was born in London (21 February 1710–17 October 1781). Hawke joined the navy in February 1720 and was promoted to rear admiral for his distinguished service against the French in the War of the Austrian Succession (1740–48). In October 1747, he captured six French warships in a reportedly brilliant action that took place off the coast of Brittany. His famous naval victory in 1759 put an end to French plans to invade Great Britain during the Seven Years' War (1756–63). Hawke also served as First Lord of the Admiralty between 1766 and 1771, during which time he oversaw the mobilization of the British navy during the 1770 Falklands crisis, a dispute with Spain (backed by France) over ownership of the islands which effectively became a non-military political standoff.

'Lord Nelson' (LN) class 4-6-0 BR No 30860 LORD HAWKE is seen at Eastleigh (71A) in July 1962, just a month before being withdrawn. *Hugh Ballantyne/Rail Photoprints*

30861 LORD ANSON (SR No 861) entered SR service September 1929, coupled with a 5000 gallon/5 ton tender. Withdrawn from BR service October 1962, cut up November 1962.

George Anson, 1st Baron Anson PC, FRS, RN was born in Staffordshire (23 April 1697–6 June 1762). Anson hailed from a wealthy Staffordshire family, of that name. He is perhaps best remembered for his circumnavigation of the globe and his role overseeing the Royal Navy during the Seven Years' War. During his time in office Anson instituted a series of reforms to the Royal Navy. In 1744 he joined the Admiralty Board and from June 1751 until November 1756 and also from 1757 until his death he was First Lord of the Admiralty. Among his reforms were the transfer of the Marines from Army to Navy authority, uniforms for commissioned officers, devising a way to effectively get superannuated Captains and Admirals to retire on half pay and submitting a revision of the Articles of War to Parliament, which reportedly tightened discipline throughout the navy.

Anson's memorial at St. Michael and All Angels Church in Colwich, Staffordshire. *Keith Langston Collection*

'Lord Nelson' (LN) class 4-6-0 BR No 30861 LORD ANSON is seen with a down Bournemouth service at Waterloo station in 1949, the locomotive was then resplendent in newly painted lime green livery, note the words BRITISH RAILWAYS on the tender. *C.R.L. Coles-Dave Cobbe Collection/Rail Photoprints*

30862 LORD COLLINGWOOD (SR No 862) entered SR service October 1929, coupled with a 5000 gallon/5 ton tender. Withdrawn from BR service October 1962, cut up November 1962.

Cuthbert Collingwood, 1st Baron Collingwood born Newcastle Upon Tyne (26 September 1748–7 March 1810) was a notable partner with Lord Nelson during several of the British victories of the Napoleonic wars, and frequently as Nelson's successor in various commands.

When not at sea he resided at Collingwood House in the town of Morpeth which lies some 15 miles north of Newcastle upon Tyne and also at Chirton Hall in Chirton, now North Shields. The Maritime Warfare School of the Royal Navy is commissioned as HMS *Collingwood*, it is home to training for warfare, weapon engineering and communications disciplines. A statue erected in his honour overlooks the River Tyne in the town of Tynemouth, at the foot of which are some of the surviving cannon from one of his commands HMS *Royal Sovereign*.

'Lord Nelson' (LN) class 4-6-0 BR No 30862 LORD RODNEY stands at Eastleigh with the 2.05pm service to Bournemouth Central, on 19 September 1959. *Hugh Ballantyne/Rail Photoprints*

30863 LORD RODNEY (SR No 863) entered SR service October 1929, coupled with a 5000 gallon/5 ton tender. Withdrawn from BR service February 1962, cut up March 1962.

George Brydges Rodney, 1st Baron Rodney, KB (baptised 13 February 1718–24 May 1792) was a British naval officer. He is best known for his commands in the American War of Independence. It is often claimed that he was the commander to have pioneered the naval battle tactic of 'breaking the line'. Some historians reportedly considered Rodney to be a controversial figure, accused of having an overriding obsession with the collection of prize monies. Rodney's victory at the Battle of the Saintes in April 1782, ended the French threat to Jamaica. On returning to Britain, Rodney was made a peer and was awarded an annual pension of £2,000.

'Lord Nelson' (LN) class 4-6-0 SR No 863 LORD RODNEY is seen in fine order, and with a young cleaner hard at work, whilst in the company of a sister locomotive at Stewarts Lane depot in March 1939. *Mike Morant Collection*

30864 SIR MARTIN FROBISHER (SR No 864) entered SR service November 1929, coupled with a 5000 gallon/5 ton tender. Withdrawn from BR service January 1962, cut up March 1962.

Sir Martin Frobisher (c. 1535/1539–15 November 1594) was an accomplished seaman and privateer. He made three voyages to the New World looking for the illusive Northwest Passage. He landed in north-eastern Canada, around Resolution Island and the accordingly named Frobisher Bay celebrates that fact. On his second voyage, Frobisher found what he thought was gold ore and carried 200 tons of it home on three ships, where initial assaying determined it to be worth a profit of £5.2 per ton. Thus encouraged, Frobisher returned to Canada with an even larger fleet and dug several mines around Frobisher Bay. He then carted 1,350 tons of the ore back where it was, together with the earlier consignment, found to actually be worthless iron pyrite (Fools Gold). He was later knighted for his service in repelling the Spanish Armada in 1588.

'Lord Nelson' (LN) class 4-6-0 SR No 859 LORD HOOD (became BR 30859) is seen prior to departing from Waterloo in this atmospheric 1940 image. *Mike Morant Collection*

'Lord Nelson' (LN) class 4-6-0 BR No 30864 SIR MARTIN FROBISHER is seen with a boat train passing Byfleet signal box, circa 1949. *Rail Photoprints Collection*

30865 SIR JOHN HAWKINS (SR No 865) entered SR service November 1929, coupled with a 5000 gallon/5 ton tender. Withdrawn from BR service May 1961, cut up August 1961.

Sir John Hawkins was born in Plymouth (c.1532–12 November 1595) he was a naval commander, navigator and administrator and additionally a merchant, shipbuilder, and privateer. He styled himself 'Captain General' as the General of both his own flotillas of ships and those of the Royal Navy. Hawkins was the chief architect of the 'Elizabethan Navy'. As treasurer and controller (1577 and 1589 respectively) of the Royal Navy, Hawkins rebuilt older ships and helped design the faster ships that engaged the Spanish Armada in 1588. His death, and that of his cousin and mentee, Sir Francis Drake heralded the decline of the Royal Navy for decades, before its recovery and eventual dominance again doubtless helped by the propaganda of the Navy's earlier glory days under his leadership.

'Lord Nelson' (LN) class 4-6-0 SR No 865 SIR JOHN HAWKINS (BR 30865) is seen in malachite green livery during 1947, precise location unknown. *Rail Photoprints Collection*

Class details

'LN' Class SR Lord Nelson 6P reclassified 7P in 1951	4-6-0	16 built 1926/29 Eastleigh	Driving Wheel 6ft 7ins dia. Loco No 30859 experimentally fitted with smaller driving wheel in 1929 (TE 35300lbf)	4 – cylinders Walschaert piston valves	Working BP 220psi Superheated Tractive effort 33510lbf

'0458' class 0-4-0ST, Southampton Dock Company/LSWR/SR/BR

Former London & South Western Railway/Southern Railway 0-4-0ST LSWR Nos 458 and later No 3458 IRONSIDE is seen as British Railways (BR) No 30458 whilst next to the turntable at Guildford shed (70C) circa 1953. *Mike Morant Collection*

30458 IRONSIDE built by Hawthorn Leslie in 1890 for the Southampton Dock Company (SDC), the 0-4-0ST became an LSWR engine in 1892, a Southern Railway locomotive in 1922 and became BR No 30458 in 1948, BR power rating 0F. This was one of two such locomotives supplied to the SDC; sister engine No 457 (later 734) was withdrawn for scrapping in 1945. No 30458 was withdrawn from Guildford depot in June 1945 and cut up in the September of that year.

Note. Evidently No 3458 should have been renumbered by the SR in the 30564, but by pure coincidence the number 30458 was available because of a war casualty in the 'T14' class. The 'T14' locomotive (No 458) suffered irreparable damage when a German bombing raid scored a direct hit on Nine Elms locomotive depot in 1940.

IRONSIDE. The Ironsides were troopers in the Parliamentarian cavalry formed by English political leader Oliver Cromwell in the 17th century, during the English Civil War. The name came from 'Old Ironsides', one of Oliver Cromwell's well known nicknames. King Edmund II was also referred to as 'Edmund Ironside' circa 1016.

Class Details

'0458' class Southampton Dock Company	0-4-0ST	Total 2 built Hawthorne Leslie 1890	Driving Wheel 3ft 2ins dia	2 cylinders Stephenson Slide valves	Working BP 120psi Tractive effort 7730lbf

Oliver Cromwell's statue at Bridgefoot, Warrington in Cheshire
is located in the grounds of the Old Academy. *Michael Ely*

Ex Plymouth, Devonport & South Western Junction Railway 0-6-2T No 757 LORD ST LEVAN is seen as BR No 30758, complete with Plymouth Friary (72D) shedplate whilst at Eastleigh in July 1956. *Rail Photoprints Collection*

30758 LORD ST LEVAN, built by Hawthorn Leslie in 1907 for the Plymouth, Devonport & South Western Railway (PDSWJ). The 0-6-2T later became an LSWR engine and a Southern Railway locomotive in 1922, and consequently became BR No 30758 in 1948. This was one of two such locomotives supplied to the PDSWJ the other being No 758 (BR No 30757), withdrawn and cut up in December 1957. No 30758 was withdrawn in December 1956 and cut up in February 1957.

When the London & South Western Railway acquired the Hawthorne Leslie & Co built 0-6-2T locomotives in 1922 they became numbers LSWR Nos 757 and 758. The outside cylinder slide valve engines were given an original BR 1MT power rating which was reclassified as 1P2F in 1953. It was the SR's original intention to buy further locomotives of the class but the rebuilding of the 'E1' class (E1R) made that unnecessary.

Lord St. Levan/Baron St. Levan. The St. Levan family name has historic and present day associations with St. Michaels Mount in Cornwall. At least two from the family line had strong military connections. The second Baron St. Levan, John Townshend St. Aubyn was a Colonel and Honorary Brigadier-General in the Grenadier Guards. The fourth Baron St. Levan, John Francis

No 30758 is seen at Eastleigh (71A) in October 1956. *Hugh Ballantyne/ Rail Photoprints*

Arthur St. Aubyn served with the Royal Navy at Dunkirk and later commanded the minesweeper *Prospect* during the Arctic Convoy period of World War II, he was awarded the Distinguished Service Cross (DSC) in 1942.

'757' class Plymouth, Devonport & South Western Railway	0-6-2T	Total 2 built Hawthorne Leslie 1907	Driving Wheel 4ft 0ins dia	2 cylinders Stephenson Slide valves	Working BP 170psi Tractive effort 18495lbf

Southern Railway ex LSWR 'N15' King Arthur class 4-6-0

British Railways took into stock 74 of this 4-6-0 class, the design of which is jointly credited to London & South Western Railway (LSWR) engineer Robert Urie and Southern Railway (SR) engineer R.E.L Maunsell. The locomotives were introduced between 1918 and 1927, with 44 locomotives being built at Eastleigh Works, and 30 locomotives by the Glasgow contractors North British Locomotive Co Ltd (NBL). They were allocated BR numbers in the series 30448–30457, 30736–30755 and 30763–30806, the Glasgow built engines were commonly and collectively known as the 'Scotch Arthurs'. They were originally designed and built for use as express passenger locomotives.

All of the class carried names associated with Arthurian Legend and were not actually allocated names with a military connection. However, the class is included because six of the 'N15' class locomotives shared names with a class of Royal Fleet Auxiliary, Landing Ship Logistics, designated the 'Round Table Class'. The locomotive nameplates were of a straight design placed centrally on the shallow combined wheel splasher.

Urie

Robert Wallace Urie (1854–1937) was a Scottish born locomotive engineer who was the last Chief Mechanical Engineer (CME) of the London & South Western Railway (L&SWR).

Having been apprenticed to several private locomotive manufacturers Urie then joined the Caledonian Railway (CR) and there served under Dugald Drummond as Chief Draughtsman and later St. Rollox Works Manager. In 1897 he moved with Drummond to join the L&SWR where Urie became works manager at Nine Elms, London. In 1909 he was transferred to the 'new' works at Eastleigh. Following the death of Dugald Drummond in 1912, Urie became Chief Mechanical Engineer until his own retirement in 1923. He died on 6 March 1937 at Largs, Ayrshire.

'Round Table Class', Landing Ship Logistics

In December 1961 the Ministry of Transport placed an order for a new class of six 6,000-ton military supply vessels. The first of the class was launched in June 1963 and the last in December 1966. The ships had both bow and stern doors leading onto the main vehicle deck, making them 'Roll-on-Roll-off' (Ro-Ro vessels), combined with ramps that led to upper and lower vehicle decks. Built to a shallow draught design they could beach themselves and use the bow doors for speedy unloading of troops and equipment. The ships had helicopter landing pads on both the upper vehicle deck and also behind the superstructure.

The ships were operated and managed by the British-India Steam Navigation Company for the Royal Army Service Corps until January 1970, then were transferred to the Royal Fleet Auxiliary (RFA). One vessel, *Sir Galahad*, was lost during the Falklands War, while another, *Sir Tristram*, was badly damaged in that conflict. The former was replaced by a new, 8,861GT vessel of the same name, while the latter was rebuilt and returned to service. All of the vessels in this class were replaced by new vessels of the 'Bay Class', with *Sir Bedivere* being the last to leave active service in 2008.

The flag which was flown by British Army ships of the Royal Logistic Corps. *Philip Ronan*

SR N15 class 'King Arthur' 4-6-0 BR No 30448 SIR TRISTRAM (SR No 448) is seen at Eastleigh, in ex-works condition. Reportedly the locomotive was renumbered into the BR 'King Arthur' series during July 1948. Note the LSWR style 8-wheel so called 'Watercart' tender and early BR logo. *Mike Morant Collection*

30448 SIR TRISTRAM (SR No 448) built at Eastleigh Works entered SR service May 1925 coupled with a 5000 gallon/ 5 ton tender. Withdrawn by BR August 1960 cut up September 1960.

RFA Sir Tristram, pennant No L3505, was built at the Tyneside yard of Hawthorn Leslie, at Hebburn. The keel was laid down on 14 March 1966 and the vessel was launched on 12 December 1966 and then commissioned on 14 September 1967. The ship was initially operated for the British Army by the British-India Steam Navigation Company, prior to being transferred to the Royal Fleet Auxiliary in 1970. In 1977 the vessel was used as a guest ship for the Queen's Silver Jubilee Fleet Review at Spithead in the Solent.

On 8 June 1982, during the Falklands war with Argentina, *Sir Tristram,* and her sister ship *Sir* Galahad, were attacked by planes of the Argentine Air Force whilst transporting men and equipment at Fitzroy Cove in the Falkland Islands. At approx 14.00 hrs local time the landing ship was strafed with bullets by the attacking aircraft and two crew members were killed. During the attack a 500lb bomb penetrated the deck but failed to explode immediately, thus giving time for the crew to be evacuated. The bomb later exploded and the vessel was declared abandoned. Following the conflict, the severely damaged vessel was transported back to the UK and rebuilt, re-entering active service in 1985. *Sir Tristram* then saw further tours of duty which included taking part in the 2003 invasion of Iraq before being de-commissioned on 17 December 2005. At the time of writing the vessel was reportedly still in use as a training facility for the Special Forces Group.

SR N15 class 'King Arthur' 4-6-0 BR No 30448 SIR TRISTRAM (SR No 448) is seen at Exmouth Junction (72A). Note that the locomotive at that time is coupled with a later version Maunsell 4-wheel tender, complete with a post 1950-but pre 1956, 'Cycling Lion' logo. *Mike Morant Collection*

30451 SIR LAMORAK (SR No 451) built at Eastleigh Works entered SR service June 1925 coupled with a 5000 gallon/ 5 ton tender. Withdrawn by BR June 1962 cut up June 1962.

RFA Sir Lamorak, pennant No L3532 was a temporarily chartered 'Roll-on Roll-off' (Ro-Ro) ferry of the Royal Fleet Auxiliary. It was procured to fill a gap caused by damage to and loss of *Round Table* class landing ships during the Falklands War. This vessel was built in Norway and launched in May 1972 entering service in the September of that year as *Anu* and operated as a Ro-Ro ferry out of Helsinki. After several years of ferry and charter work, which included stints on Channel Island and UK-Ireland routes the ship was acquired in February 1982 by the RFA. She was refitted and then renamed *Sir Lamorak*, and commissioned on 11 March 1983. The vessel was purchased in order to transport troops and equipment during the aforementioned Falklands conflict. However, the vessel was found to be unsuitable for use in South Atlantic waters and transferred to other military supply work in the North Sea. *Sir Lamorak* was decommissioned on 20 January 1986 and returned to the previous owners, she was renamed *Merchant Trader* in late 1986. More name changes followed and they included *Mols Trader* in 1987, *Mads Mols* in 1988, *Pride of Portsmouth* in 1989, *Norman Commodore* in 1991, and *Fjardvagen* in 1995. In late 2013 the vessel was reportedly still in service and operating as a ferry in Finnish waters.

SR Urie development of a N15 class 'King Arthur' 4-6-0 BR No 30451 SIR LAMORAK (SR No 451) is seen at Eastleigh (71A), in June 1962. The straight rectangular nameplate incorporating the class annotation can be clearly seen on the splasher over the central driving wheel. The locomotive is coupled to a Maunsell 4-wheeled tender, complete with a post 1956 'Ferret and Dartboard' logo. *Rail Photoprints Collection*

30455 SIR LANCELOT (SR No 455) built at Eastleigh Works entered SR service March 1925 coupled with a 5000 gallon/5 ton tender. Withdrawn by BR April 1959 cut up May 1959.

RFA Sir Lancelot, pennant No L3532 was built on the Clyde by Fairfield Shipbuilding & Engineering of Govan, this vessel was the prototype of the '*Round Table Class*' of landing ships. The keel was laid down in March 1962 and the vessel was launched on 26 June 1963 and commissioned on 16 January 1964. The ship was initially operated for the British Army by the British-India Steam Navigation Company, prior to being transferred to the Royal Fleet Auxiliary in 1970. On 24 May 1982, whilst in San Carlos Water during the Falklands conflict, she was hit by a 1,000lb Argentine bomb, which penetrated her starboard side but failed to explode. Following the cessation of hostilities and after repairs, she operated in Falkland Islands waters before returning to Portsmouth.

Sir Lancelot was decommissioned and sold in 1989 to a South African company who renamed her *Lowland Lancer* and was used as a Channel ferry initially on the Weymouth to Cherbourg route, before becoming a floating casino. The vessel was purchased by the Republic of Singapore Navy in 1992, and was re-commissioned as RSS *Perseverance* (L206) in 1994. She was sold again in 2003, to Glenn Defence Marine Asia, which renamed the ship *Glenn Braveheart*. In early 2008, the ship was sold for breaking up as scrap, and taken to Bangladesh.

30456 SIR GALAHAD (SR No 456) built at Eastleigh Works entered SR service March 1925 coupled with a 5000 gallon/5 ton tender. Withdrawn by BR May 1960 cut up May 1960.

RFA *Sir Galahad,* pennant No L3005 was built on the Clyde by Alexander Stephen and Sons. The keel was laid down in February 1965 and the vessel was launched on 19 April 1966. She was first managed for the British Army by the British-India Steam Navigation Company, before being transferred in 1970 to the RFA.

Sir Galahad was active during the Falklands War. On 24 May 1982 in San Carlos Water she was attacked by aircraft of the Argentine Air Force and was hit by a 1,000lb bomb which failed to detonate. After removal of the unexploded bomb, she carried out supply runs along with RFA *Sir Percivale*. On 8 June 1982 while preparing to unload soldiers from the Welsh Guards in Port Pleasant, (off Fitzroy) together with RFA *Sir Tristram*, the *Sir Galahad* was again attacked by the Argentine Air Force and she was hit by bombs and set alight. A total of 48 soldiers and crewman were killed in the explosions and subsequent fire. Her captain, Philip Roberts waited until the last minute to abandon ship, he was subsequently awarded the DSO for his leadership and courage. Additionally, Seaman Chiu Yiu-Nam was awarded the George Medal for rescuing ten men trapped in the bowels of the ship. Guardsman Simon Weston OBE was also amongst the survivors of the attack. The hulk was later towed out to sea and sunk being designated an official war grave. A replacement ship entered service in 1988, carrying the same name and pennant number.

The ship's bell from the ill fated RFA Sir Galahad which now hangs proudly in the Falklands Chapel at Pangbourne College, near Reading in Berkshire. An annual service of remembrance is held in the Memorial Chapel, for information see www.falklands-chapel.org.uk/annual-service/

https://www.youtube.com/watch?v=c-_l3ezW0l4
Falklands War – San Carlos Landings 1982 Falklands – A Soldiers Story.

SR 'N15' class Urie development of a Maunsell 'King Arthur' 4-6-0 BR No 30456 SIR GALAHAD (SR No 456). The locomotive is seen in August 1956 whilst shunting SR passenger stock at Clapham Junction carriage sheds, note the original design double bogie 8 wheel 'watercart' tender, in this instance the coal is piled above the height of the locomotive's cab roof. This detail filled image of the carriage sidings was taken from the footbridge; note also the main running lines and platforms to the left and the imposing structure of the Granada Cinema. *Mike Morant Collection*

30457 SIR BEDIVERE (SR No 457) built at Eastleigh Works entered SR service April 1925 coupled with a 5000 gallon/5 ton tender. Withdrawn by BR May 1961 cut up July 1961.

RFA Sir Bedivere, pennant No L3004 was built by Hawthorn Leslie of Hebburn, on the River Tyne. The keel was laid down in October 1966 and the vessel was launched on 20 July 1967.

She was first managed for the British Army by the British-India Steam Navigation Company, before being transferred in 1970 to the RFA.

Sir Bedivere was active during the Falklands War. The ship was slightly damaged on 24 May 1982 when a bomb from an Argentine aircraft glanced off her superstructure, whilst she was lying in San Carlos Water. On 16 November 1982 she returned from the Falklands with the bodies of 64 British Forces (52 soldiers, 11 Royal Marines, and a Chinese laundryman) whose families had requested that their remains be returned for burial. The vessel was modernised and lengthened in 1994, thereafter seeing service in the Mediterranean, the Gulf and Sierra Leone and then decommissioned in February 2008. After a major refit the vessel was sold to the Brazilian Navy and commissioned by them in May 2009.

30766 SIR GERAINT (SR No 766) built in Glasgow by the North British Locomotive Company (NBL) entered SR service May 1925 coupled with a 5000 gallon/5 ton tender. Withdrawn by BR December 1958 cut up January 1959. The locomotive was a so called 'Scotch Arthur'. (SR No 766) built in Glasgow by the North British Locomotive Company (NBL) entered SR service May 1925 coupled with a 5000 gallon/5 ton tender. Withdrawn by BR December 1958 cut up January 1959.

RFA Sir Geraint, pennant No L3037 was ordered in April 1964 and built on the Clyde by Alexander Stephens and Sons of Linthouse, Glasgow. The keel of L3037 was laid down in June 1965 and the vessel was launched on 26 January 1967. Interestingly it was the shipyard that the Scottish entertainer and TV personality Billy Connolly CBE served his apprenticeship as a boilermaker/welder. She was first managed for the British Army by the British-India Steam Navigation Company, before being transferred to the RFA in 1970.

Sir Geraint was active during the Falklands War (1982) and was decommissioned in May 2003. Thereafter the vessel was sold into commercial use and renamed *Sir G,* before being cut up for scrap, reportedly in India, during December 2005.

North British (NBL) built SR 'N15' class, a so called Scotch Arthur, 4-6-0 SR No 766 (BR 30766) SIR GERAINT is seen in Southern Railway (SR) livery at Dover Marine, date unknown. *Mike Morant Collection*

Urie development of SR 'N15' class 'King Arthur' 4-6-0 BR No 30766 SIR GERAINT (SR No766) is seen on Sole Street Bank with a Kent Coast service, May 1953. *Dave Cobbe Collection/Rail Photoprints*

North British built SR 'N15' class 4-6-0 BR No 30772 SIR PERCIVALE (SR No 772) is seen near Holmsley in the New Forest, with a Ringwood bound service, 1954. *Rail Photoprints Collection*

30772 SIR PERCIVALE (SR No 772) built in Glasgow by the North British Locomotive Company (NBL) entered SR service June 1925 coupled with a 5000 gallon/5 ton tender. Withdrawn by BR September 1961 cut up December 1961.

RFA Sir Percivale, pennant No L3036 was built by Swan Hunter & Company of Wallsend.

The keel was laid down in May 1966 and the vessel was launched on 4 October 1967. She was first managed for the British Army by the British-India Steam Navigation Company, before being transferred in 1970 to the RFA. *Sir Percivale* was active during the Falklands War, but unlike her sister ships in that conflict, she emerged unscathed. She was the British first vessel to re-enter Stanley Harbour. Thereafter the ship saw service in the Gulf, the Adriatic, and 'Operation *Ocean Wave 97*' and was present during the handover of Hong Kong. *Sir Percivale* was decommissioned on 17 August 2004 and was 'laid up alongside' at Marchwood Military Port, Southampton. *Sir Percivale* remained at the Sea Mounting Centre (SMC) until 0058hrs, 13 December 2009 when she was towed to Liverpool for scrapping.

North British built SR 'N15' class 4-6-0 BR No 30772 SIR PERCIVALE (SR No 772) is seen with a local service near New Malden, circa 1958. Note the electrified '3rd' rails. *Mike Morant Collection*

N15 class basic Specifications

'N15' Class LSWR 'King Arthur' class 5P	4-6-0	74 built 1918/27 30 at Eastleigh and 44 at NBL Glasgow	Driving Wheel 6ft 7ins dia	2 – cylinders Locos 30736-30754 fitted with modified cylinders in 1928 Tractive effort 23915lbf Walschaert piston valves	Locos 30736-30755 working BP 180psi Tractive effort 26245lbf Locos 30453–30457, 30448–30452, 30763–30792 and 30793–30806 working BP 200psi Tractive effort 25320lbf All Superheated

Preserved Re-Built Bulleid 'Battle of Britain' class Pacific No 34059
SIR ARCHIBALD SINCLAIR is seen on Santa Special duty at Holy Well
on the Bluebell Railway during the winter of 2009. *Paul Pettitt*

Bulleid Light Pacific locomotives and the Battle of Britain

The Battle of Britain

In order that Hitler's Germany could successfully invade Britain, or indeed alternatively force Britain to the negotiating table, the Nazis had first to gain control of the skies over Britain and of course the English Channel.

The Battle of Britain was the first major campaign to be fought entirely by air forces. At the start of the battle the Royal Air Force reportedly had 531 serviceable fighters out of a total of 609, and in reserve another 289 aircraft. The German would-be invaders had in total 4,539 aircraft. The uninitiated observer would be right to assume that the odds were very much stacked in the favour of Germany.

But as history later recorded those odds were overturned, and mainly thanks to the bravery and selfless efforts of the RAF, Hitler was forced to call off his planned invasion of Britain. Germany's "Operation Sealion" therefore did not achieve its stated aims and when the Nazis' most senior commander, Field Marshal von Runstedt, was asked after the surrender of his country, which battle he regarded as the most decisive, he replied: "The Battle of Britain".

The British Railway authorities chose to give a selected number of their new Bulleid Light Pacific (4-6-2) streamlined (air-smoothed casing) steam locomotives (introduced 1945–1951), names with connections to the aforementioned historically important air battle.

Those locomotives initially operated over the Southern Railway (SR) and then the Southern Region of British Railways (SR-BR). They were of a distinctive design and a good number were later rebuilt and served almost to the end of the steam era.

There are 9 'Battle of Britain' class locomotives preserved, in their embodiment Churchill's tribute to 'The Few' still lives on.
Keith Langston Collection

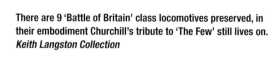

Southern Railway Bulleid 'Battle of Britain' class Pacific (4-6-2)

Preserved Bulleid Light Pacific Southern Region 'Battle of Britain' class locomotive BR No 34070 MANSTON is seen climbing away from Corfe Castle station, on the Swanage Railway. The impressive castle ruins complement the picture. *Paul Pettitt*

The 'Battle of Britain' class locomotive names are significantly important because they commemorate a dark time in Britain's history, when against enormous odds the country fought for her very existence. Indeed, if the heroic acts of 'The Few' had failed during the summer of 1940 you would certainly be reading a very different history of those events. It is no exaggeration to say that in September 1940 the British nation hovered on the very brink of extinction!

O.V.S. Bulleid

Bulleid was born in Invercargill New Zealand on 19 September 1882 but his family later moved to the UK, and his formal education was undertaken at Accrington Technical School in Lancashire. His introduction to locomotive engineering was with the Great Northern Railway (GNR), he joined their Doncaster Works as an apprentice in 1901 and entered their employ 'proper' in 1906. In 1908 Bullied went to France to work as Chief Draughtsman, and then Assistant Works Manager, for French Westinghouse Company. He then had a three-year spell with the UK Board of Trade as Chief Mechanical and Electrical Engineer for British Exhibits.

In 1912 he began his employment with the North Eastern Railway (NER) as Principal Assistant to the great N.H. Gresley. In 1923 'grouping' saw the GNR become the London & North Eastern Railway (LNER), following that change Bullied continued to serve under Gresley in the same role. Thus he clocked up a total of 22 years working with the man whose name became synonymous with the successful streamlining of steam locomotives. Bulleid was renowned for his flair and innovation and put both facets to good use at the LNER during the design and building of the streamlined 'Silver Jubilee' coaches.

In September 1937 Bulleid joined the Southern Railway (SR) and began working alongside his predecessor R.E.L. Maunsell. His first few years in post were spent effecting design improvements to locomotives of the existing SR fleet. When, in 1939, the Southern Railway board identified their urgent need for a new fast heavy passenger locomotive they turned to their new Chief Mechanical Engineer (CME).

Bulleid had previously served with Nigel Gresley (later Sir Nigel) at the London North Eastern Railway (LNER) and as Principal Assistant to Gresley he had played a big part in the development of the streamlined 'A4' Pacific class of engines. Perhaps unsurprisingly Bulleid also chose a streamlined, or as the SR termed it 'air smoothed casing', design for his Pacific locomotives.

Even though final design and building was slowed down by the onset of WWII Bulleid did gain permission to commence building his first unique heavy 'Merchant Navy' class 8P 4-6-2 class locomotives. Innovation was very much the Bulleid way and his 'Pacific' designs included not only the aforementioned streamlining but also incorporated chain driven valve gear which was immersed in an oil bath. Other innovations included American style 'boxpok' type wheels, electric lighting and an all welded construction steel firebox.

The Bulleid Firth Brown wheel was a locomotive wheel developed for the Southern Railway in the late 1930s. It was a disc wheel, in contrast to the usual spoked wheels in general use by British railway companies. The wheel was designed by Oliver Bulleid and developed by the steel company Firth Brown of Sheffield. *Keith Langston Collection*

 https://www.youtube.com/watch?v=sFqZwwJgHd4
Bulleid Pacific Day – Swanage Railway.

After nationalisation Oliver Bulleid, who in 1949 was awarded a CBE, went to work for British Railways as Chief Mechanical Engineer of BR Southern Region, but the relationship was short lived. He resigned from BR and took up the post of Consultant Engineer (later becoming C.M.E) with Córas Iompair Éireann (CIÉ) the Irish State Railways. Whilst there, in addition to experimenting with a turf (peat) burning steam locomotive, he actually presided over the phasing out of steam traction, and the introduction of diesel traction. Bulleid retired in 1958 and went to live in Devon, he later moved to Malta the 'George Cross Island', where he died on 25 April 1970.

Bulleid Light Pacific Locomotives

Following the success and introduction of the '8P' Merchant Navy class pacific locomotives (1941-1949) the Southern Railway identified the need for an express locomotive with greater route availability. To fulfil that need Bulleid designed a 'scaled down' version of the air smoothed 'MN' class Pacifics, that type became known as the West Country/Battle of Britain class 7P5F 4-6-2 engines also known as 'Light Pacifics'. 'BB' class locomotives 34049-34070 (BR) were built with 8ft 6ins wide cabs and numbers 34071-34090 and 34109–34110 (BR) were built with 9ft wide cabs.

The smaller, lighter and less powerful Bulleid Light Pacifics eventually totalled 110 locomotives of which 44 locos were designated as 'Battle of Britain' class and 66 were 'West Country' class. Although almost identical in looks the 'Battle of Britain' class however did have minor modifications to cab and tender contours to enable them to work through the restricted tunnels of the Tonbridge–Hastings Line (which they never actually did on a regular basis). The majority of Light Pacifics (all of the 'Battle of Britain' locomotives) were built at Brighton but 6 'West Country' class locomotives, from the last batch ordered, were constructed at Eastleigh.

The first 'Battle of Britain' locomotive BR No 34049 (21C149) emerged from Brighton Works in December 1946 and production continued until BR No 34070 (21C170) became the last to emerge from the works under Southern Railway ownership, in October 1947. The first 'Battle of Britain' locomotive to be built under British Railways ownership, BR No 34071, emerged in April 1948, the last 'Light Pacific' (and 'Battle of Britain' Class) to be built was BR No 34110 which entered traffic in January 1951.

Bulleid Light Pacific 'Battle of Britain' class SR No s21C149 (BR 34079) ANTI-AIRCRAFT COMMAND is pictured at Exmouth Junction shed (72A) in SR livery. Note that the allocated number has an additional 's' prefix and that the tender carries the words BRITISH RAILWAYS but the smoke box door has an SR roundel. Those factors combine to make this a very rare image; it was taken between 13 March 1948 and 18 February 1949. Immediately after railway nationalisation in 1948 the Bulleid numbering system was for a short period retained on some SR Pacifics, but with the addition of the 's' prefix. *Mike Morant Collection*

Locomotives of both classes of Bulleid Pacific were extensively rebuilt under British Railways and the programme to rebuild 60 of the light Pacifics commenced in 1957. Essentially the rebuilding centred on the removal of the 'air smoothed casing' and the replacement of the chain driven valve gear with more conventional Walschaerts equipment.

After the addition of square smoke deflectors some observers have since commented upon the similarity in looks between the rebuilt Bulleid 4-6-2 locomotives and the BR Standard Pacifics. BR No 34059 SIR ARCHIBALD SINCLAIR is seen at the Bluebell Railway in October 2009. *Paul Pettitt*

Battle of Britain class – a comparison of locomotive design styles

Preserved Bulleid Light Pacific 'Battle of Britain' class BR No 34081 92 SQUADRON is seen at the Bluebell Railway. The locomotive has been faithfully restored after having been withdrawn by BR (August 1964) in Bulleid's original 'air smoothed casing' design. *Paul Pettitt*

Preserved Bulleid Light Pacific 'Battle of Britain' class BR No 34053 SIR KEITH PARK is seen at the Severn Valley Railway. The locomotive was re-built in the un-streamlined form by British Railways (BR) in November 1958, and withdrawn in October 1965. *John Chalcraft*

Our railways under attack

Whilst it is right and proper to remember the fallen of the Battle of Britain, and indeed World War II, let us also remember the fallen amongst railway personnel. The Southern Railway network was right in the front line during the decisive Battle of Britain. There were many attacks on railway installations and casualties were high, but none of the raids stopped the trains running permanently. In addition to moving troops, war materials etc the railways were also busy evacuating young people to safer areas, as the intensive German bombing (Blitz) of our cities intensified. Those who toiled selflessly to keep Britain's trains running also made an outstanding contribution to the war effort, thus the eventual victory was also their well deserved reward.

The Battle

The air war was fought not over some distant battlefield but in full view of a large section of the civilian population of Southern England. At the onset of the Battle of Britain the Luftwaffe had a vastly superior number of aircraft when compared to the Royal Air Force and the German High Command expected to easily destroy the RAF's planes 'on the ground'. To that end their battle plan started with an attack on allied shipping, coastal military installations and ports, then swiftly moved on to attack airfields and radar installations. The watching, and perhaps unknowing population, were soon to suffer horribly at the hands of the Luftwaffe as later the German commanders switched their incessant air attacks from military installations and commenced attacking many of Britain's cities and towns together with their mainly civilian populations.

https://www.youtube.com/watch?v=G4BVzYGeF0M
Their Finest Hour-Churchill Speech.

SR Bulleid 'Battle of Britain' class Light Pacific locomotive BR No 34051 WINSTON CHURCHILL is seen preparing to leave Axminster in May 1963 with a 3 coach westbound local service for Exeter. *David Anderson*

7

8

KEY
1. People shelter from the bombs in London's Aldwych underground station.
2. Messerschmitt 'BF 110' bomber, nicknamed the Flying Shark, over the English Channel.
3. The railway infrastructure sustained repeated damage during the Blitz, but the trains never stopped running.
4. A great many British cities were extensively bombed; this is Manchester Victoria station after an air raid.
5. Wartime firefighters at work during the Blitz.
6. Londons's Windmill Theatre carried on with musical and variety shows right through the bombing. Between shows the artists lived and ate in their dressing rooms, often sleeping on mattresses in the theatre dressing rooms.
7. The Luftwaffe seen loading a bomb inscribed with a message for Mr. Churchill.
8. Workers survey bomb damage at a removal depot in London.
9. Many young people were evacuated by rail from vulnerable areas of cities and lodged out with families in safer country areas.

https://www.youtube.com/watch?v=PHknZf4AXKc
The Bombing of Coventry.

9

On 11 June 1940 Britain's war time leader Winston Churchill addressed a very sombre House of Commons. The spirit of his carefully chosen words perchance formed the very rock on which modern Britain stands. Those of an age will recall that famous Chuchillian 'battle cry' which helped bind our beleaguered nation together, whilst at the same time inspiring our armed forces to perform unbelievable deeds of bravery in defence of their cherished families and beloved homeland.

Churchill said, 'The Battle for France is over. The Battle for Britain is about to begin. Upon this battle depends the survival of Christian civilization…The whole fury and might of the enemy must very soon be turned on us. Hitler knows that he will have to break us in this island or lose the war…Let us therefore brace ourselves to our duty, and so bear ourselves that, if the British Empire and its Commonwealth lasts for a thousand years, men will still say…This was their finest hour'.

Remember that the British Expeditionary Forces (BEF) had just been evacuated from the beaches of Dunkirk, suffering huge losses (27 May–5 June 1940). The Americans had not at that time entered the war and except for a small number of Commonwealth service personnel and a handful of brave European fighters, who had escaped to Britain from German occupied territories, we were truly alone. Those who stood on British soil at that time were the only ones in a position to defend it.

At the start of the battle, the German Luftwaffe had in the region of 2,500 planes that were serviceable, and in any normal day the German High Command could put over 1,600 planes in the air against Britain. The Royal Air Force on the other hand had approximately 1,200 planes on the eve of the battle, a total which included 800 Spitfire and Hurricane fighters, but reportedly only 660 of those were serviceable.

Perhaps the greatest advantage which the RAF had over the Luftwaffe was RADAR which gave the defenders early warnings of approaching enemy planes. By the spring of 1940, over fifty RADAR bases were in operation along the coast of Southern Britain. The term *RADAR* was coined in 1940 by the United States Navy as an acronym for **RA**dio **D**etection **A**nd **R**anging. The word *radar* has since entered the English language as a common noun.

Those stations were supplemented by the Royal Observer Corps (ROC) whose over 1000 observers used such basic equipment as binoculars and telescopes to search the skies for enemy aircraft. Historians consider that the real air war started on 12 August, the day the German air force made their first direct attack on the RAF. In the early battles the Luftwaffe actually lost more planes than the RAF, however by 31 August the commanders of the RAF realised that their force was near to collapse. During the last two weeks of August 1940 they had lost 295 planes and had another 170 damaged by the German attacks.

The RAF's young flyers and ground crews were often on the point of exhaustion, many carrying out five or more sorties in a day. Importantly the RAF was unable to train new aircrew at anything like the same rate at which they were being killed. The 30 and 31 August marked the worst weekend of the Battle of Britain. In fierce fighting the RAF lost another 65 aircraft and six of the seven strategic sections, which formed the important Fighter Command south east Group, were put out of action, in fact the air defences of Britain were in danger of failing.

On 24 August the Luftwaffe had dropped bombs on London; in retaliation the RAF bombed Berlin a few nights later. Hitler was furious, and on 2 September he ordered his bombers to cease attacking airfields and they instead attacked London. The intensive German Blitz of Great Britain thus began. However, that change of German strategy was fortunate for the RAF, as the sudden and unexpected respite from airfield bombings gave them time to re-equip and regroup.

EVACUATION
OF
WOMEN AND CHILDREN
FROM LONDON, Etc.

FRIDAY, 1st SEPTEMBER.

Up and Down business trains as usual, with few exceptions.

Main Line and Suburban services will be curtailed while evacuation is in progress during the day.

SATURDAY & SUNDAY,
SEPTEMBER 2nd & 3rd.

The train service will be exactly the same as on <u>Friday</u>.

Remember that there will be very few Down <u>Mid-day</u> business trains on <u>Saturday</u>.

SOUTHERN RAILWAY

A Southern Railway wartime notice.

https://www.youtube.com/watch?v=KtZema1yjOk
The First Day Of The Blitz.

Winston Churchill *"The gratitude of every home…goes out to the British airman, who undaunted by odds, unwearied in their constant challenge and mortal danger, are turning the tide of the world war by their prowess and by their devotion. Never in the field of human conflict was so much owed by so many to so few."* Memorable words which were spoken by Winston Churchill in the House of Commons at the height of the Battle of Britain, on 20 August 1940. The 15 September is celebrated annually as 'Battle of Britain Day'.

The German 'Blitz' air raid which took place on 7 September was so massive, that the sheer number of German aircraft crossing the coast led some British commanders to, albeit briefly, believe that the invasion of Britain had started. The anticipated invasion was codenamed 'Operation Sealion' by the Germans. However, the understrength, but revitalised RAF fought on as the Luftwaffe bombing raids continued, the RAF flyers were well outnumbered and yet fighting against massive odds still inflicted substantial losses upon the German attackers.

On 15 September the Germans staged a day time attack, again with a huge number of planes and with the stated intention of sweeping the RAF from the skies. Remarkably at one point in that decisive encounter, every serviceable British fighter plane was in the skies over South Eastern England. The RAF flyers often needed to land, refuel and re-arm before rejoining the battle. On the other hand, the Luftwaffe attackers were unable to refuel etc and thus were often fighting at the limit of their aircrafts' effective range. Accordingly, the German pilots had less time over their targets than they would have liked and they were frequently forced to turn tail and run for home. The tide of battle eventually started to turn in favour of Britain. In all, the RAF lost a total of 1,173 planes in the Battle of Britain, and 510 pilots and aircrew were killed. The *Luftwaffe* lost some 1,733 planes and 3,368 of their airmen were killed or captured. If the *Luftwaffe* had succeeded, Britain would doubtless have been invaded and conquered by Germany. But because the RAF held out, Great Britain survived!

The principal British aircraft

Mention of the Battle of Britain always calls to mind the famous Hurricane and Spitfire fighters locked in combat with Messerschmitt 109s, leaving a tangle of condensation trails in the skies of Southern England. The prototype Spitfire made its maiden flight from Eastleigh airport on 5 March 1936. Tragically, its designer R.J. Mitchell died in June 1937 (at the age of 42) and so did not see the fulfilment of his design. At the onset of the Battle of Britain 19 RAF squadrons had been equipped with Supermarine Spitfires; those aircraft had a reported top speed 362 mph.

Designed by Sydney Camm in 1934, the Hurricane proved to be one of the most outstanding machines in the history of military aviation. It was the first combat aircraft to exceed 300 mph in level flight and the first fighter aircraft to be fitted with eight guns. Of the total of 68 WWII 'Battle of Britain Squadrons' 36 were equipped with Hawker Hurricane aircraft, with their top speed listed as being 328 mph.

During the battle Fighter Command also had other types of aircraft at its disposal and those included Bristol Blenheim Mk 1F, Bristol Blenheim Mk IVF, Bristol Beaufighter Mk 1F, Boulton Paul Defiant Mk 1, Boulton Paul Defiant Mk II, Gloster Gladiator Mk II, Grumman Martlet Mk I and the Fairey Fulmar Mk1.

The principal German aircraft

The Messerschmitt 109 was Nazi Germany's primary fighter plane which during the Battle of Britain accompanied the 'would be' invader's bomber aircraft, in order to try and protect them from attack by the defending RAF fighter aircraft. The builders of the single engine '109' fighter claimed it capable of speeds in the region of 380 mph; it was reportedly a worthy adversary for the RAF's Spitfire and Hurricane fighters. The Luftwaffe's primary bombers during the period were the Heinkel He 111, Dornier Do 17, and Junkers Ju 88 for level bombing, and the Junkers Ju 87 *Stuka* for dive bombing attacks.

Battle of Britain Memorial Flight

The Battle of Britain Memorial Flight (BBMF) is a Royal Air Force flight which provides an aerial display group comprising an *Avro Lancaster*, a *Supermarine Spitfire* and a *Hawker Hurricane*. The aircraft are regularly seen at events commemorating the Second World War and upon British State occasions, and also at air displays throughout the United Kingdom and Europe. The flight is administratively part of No. 1 Group RAF, flying out of RAF Coningsby in Lincolnshire.

The RAF BBMF hangar is located within the boundaries of RAF Coningsby and viewing the Flight's historic aircraft at close quarters is available only by guided tour. See web site www.lincolnshire.gov.uk/bbmf

Naming the BB class locomotives

In the post war years, it was realised that the use of 'West Country' named light Pacifics would seem not a little incongruous on trains in the South Eastern Sector and the 'Battle of Britain' Class was born. Once the decision had been taken to name the 'Battle of Britain' locomotives the Southern Railway management (and later Southern Region of BR) had 71 Battle of Britain squadrons and a large number of personalities, aircraft and locations to choose from, the Air Ministry qualification being that names be chosen from those squadrons, aircraft and locations deemed to have fought in the 'Battle' under the control of Fighter Command between 00.01 hours on 10 July and 23.59 hours on 31 October 1940. In the event the railway authorities chose to name their 44 selected locomotives thus, 24 after squadrons, 8 after prominent persons, 6 after airfields, 3 after organisations, 2 after aircraft and 1 with an appropriate collective name. Brief descriptions of the chosen names give an insight into the historically important 'Battle of Britain'.

The first naming ceremonies of the class took place at Waterloo Station on 11 September 1947 when SR No 21C151 WINSTON CHURCHILL (BR 34051), SR No 21C152 LORD DOWDING (BR 34052) and SR No 21C164 FIGHTER COMMAND (BR 34064) were named, other ceremonies followed but the majority of the 'BB' class locomotives were named without ceremony. The chosen nameplate style included an appropriate crest beneath the locomotive's name mounted on the boiler cladding for originally built engines, whilst the later rebuilds carried the name and crest on a frame fixed above the running plate with the crests located above the names. Rebuilt style locomotive nameplate and crest for BR No 34090 SIR EUSTACE MISSENDEN was an exception to this rule and additionally No 34110 66 SQUADRON only carried a nameplate and no RAF squadron crest.

Original 'Battle of Britain' class name style.

Rebuilt 'Battle of Britain' class name style.

Early scrapping?

Considering the enforced fiscal prudence of 1960s the British Railways Southern Region locomotive scrapping policy looked to be out of step, if not even reckless by comparison! Having rebuilt, at a cost in the region of £13K per loco, 60 Bulleid light pacific locomotives (including 17 'Battle of Britain' class engines) between 1957 and 1961 the network operator then chose to scrap perfectly serviceable locomotives only a few years later (each loco when new cost in the region of £20K). For example, No 34109 SIR TRAFFORD LEIGH-MALLORY only worked for 3½ years after rebuilding before being withdrawn, sister loco No 34058 SIR FREDERICK PILE fared little better, being rebuilt November 1960 and withdrawn October 1964.

SR Bulleid 'Battle of Britain' class Light Pacific locomotive BR No 34086 219 SQUADRON without a tender is seen out of use at Weymouth in March 1966. Note that the locomotive is also minus a set of driving wheels and void of rods and motion, although surprisingly the nameplate and crest is still in place. No 34086 was withdrawn by BR in November 1966 having had a service life of only 17 years, 6 months and 1 day. *Brian Robbins/Rail Photoprints Collection*

https://www.youtube.com/watch?v=-IpbjLL4J9k
Steam Engines of the Southern Railway.

Preserved SR Bulleid 'Battle of Britain' class Light Pacific locomotive BR No 34067 TANGMERE is seen on charter train work, west of Bath. *Malcolm Ranieri*

https://www.youtube.com/watch?v=t6dr8Rd0ZWM
Preserved BR No 34067 TANGMERE.

Two notable London 'BB' statues

Air Chief Marshal Sir Keith Park commanded RAF squadrons that defended London and the South East from Luftwaffe attacks in 1940. The German air force commanders reportedly referred to New Zealand born Park as the 'Defender of London'.

The 2.78m (9ft) bronze statue created by sculptor Les Johnson was unveiled in Waterloo Place, Haymarket. London on the 70th anniversary of Battle of Britain Day. Wing Commander Bob Foster, 90, and Sir Keith's great-great niece, Leigh Park, unveiled the memorial.

The statue stands close to New Zealand House and faces the direction pilots would have looked while waiting for the Luftwaffe in 1940.

Air Chief Marshal Sir Keith Rodney Park GCB, KBE, MC & Bar, DFC (15 June 1892–6 February 1975) was a New Zealand soldier, First World War flying ace and Second World War Royal Air Force commander. He was in operational command during two of the most significant air battles in the European theatre in the Second World War, helping to win the Battle of Britain and the Battle of Malta.

The statue of Winston Churchill in Parliament Square, London, is a bronze sculpture of the former British Prime Minister, created by Ivor Roberts-Jones.

It is located on a spot referred to in the 1950s by Churchill as "where my statue will go". Unveiled by his widow Lady Clementine Spencer-Churchill in 1973, the unveiling was attended by the serving Prime Minister and four former Prime Ministers, and HRH Queen Elizabeth II who made a fitting speech.

The statue is 12 feet (3.7 m) high and it shows Winston Churchill standing with his hand resting on his walking stick and wearing a military greatcoat. The plinth is 8 feet (2.4 m) high with "Churchill" inscribed on it in large capital letters.

'BB' class locomotive BR No 34053 is named in honour of SIR KEITH PARK.   'BB' class locomotive BR No 34051 is named in honour of WINSTON CHURCHILL.

The Battle of Britain Monument – Victoria Embankment, London

A general view of a section of the monument.

The Battle of Britain Monument in London is a sculpture on the Victoria Embankment, overlooking the River Thames, which commemorates the British military personnel who took part in the Battle of Britain during the Second World War. The monument is made from panelled granite and bronze. It features bronze plaques that list the names of 2936 airman and ground crew from the fourteen allied countries who took part in the battle.

It was unveiled on 18 September 2005, the 65th anniversary of the Battle, by HRH Prince Charles and Camilla, Duchess of Cornwall, in the presence of many of the surviving airmen known collectively as "The Few", following the Royal Air Force Service of Thanksgiving and Rededication on Battle of Britain Sunday. This service is an annual event, the first of which took place in 1943 at St Paul's Cathedral and since has taken place in Westminster Abbey.

The sculptor of the monument is Paul Day. The statue was cast by Morris Singer & Company, which is the oldest established fine art foundry in the world and has cast many prominent statues and sculptures in London and around the world, including the lions and fountains in Trafalgar Square.

The monument utilises a panelled granite structure 25 m (82 ft) long which was originally designed as a smoke outlet for underground trains when they were powered by steam locomotives.

Two of the intricate panels which make up the monument.

Battle of Britain Memorial Trust

The National Memorial to the 'Few' at Capel-le-Ferne, on the famous white cliffs between Dover and Folkestone in Kent. Maintained by the Battle of Britain Memorial Trust, the site at Capel-le-Ferne is dedicated to Churchill's famous "Few".

The Memorial is said to inspire quiet reflection on the bravery and sacrifice shown by the aircrew – fewer than 3,000 men – who flew, fought and tragically died in that most crucial of air battles. The Christopher Foxley-Norris Memorial Wall lists the names of all those who took part in the Battle of Britain, whilst replica Spitfire and Hurricane aircraft stand nearby as a reminder of those who flew them to victory. See also www.battleofbritainmemorial.org/the-memorial/

https://www.youtube.com/watch?v=Y0t-RqjMH-A
Never in The Field of Human Conflict Was So Much Owed By So Many To So Few-Churchill.

The Locomotives

In the listing **P** denotes preserved locomotives (9 'Battle of Britain' class), **R** (plus date rebuilt) where appropriate the original Bulleid 'Continental' style numbers are shown thus (21C149) **N** denotes nameplate now held by the RAF Museum. Most of the plates were presented by British Railways (BR) to various units of the Royal Air Force. As stated earlier all of the 'BB' class Light Pacific locomotives were built at Brighton Works.

34049 ANTI-AIRCRAFT COMMAND (21C149) entered service December 1946 coupled to a 4500 gallon/5 ton capacity tender. Withdrawn by BR December 1963 cut up at Eastleigh Works June 1964.

Anti-Aircraft Command controlled the defensive anti-aircraft artillery units of the British Isles and was formed on 1 April 1939 under General Sir Alan Brooke, who was succeeded by Sir Frederick Pile, who remained in charge for the duration of the war. Its HQ was in the grounds of Bentley Priory, Stanmore in the London Borough of Harrow.

Anti-Aircraft Command badge.

Observer Corps spotter on a London rooftop.

Bulleid 'Battle of Britain' class Light Pacific BR No 34049 ANTI-AIRCRAFT COMMAND heads under Battledown Flyover (Worting Junction) with a local service to Salisbury, on 21 August 1963. *Rail Photoprints Collection*

Rebuilt Bulleid Light Pacific BR No 34050 ROYAL OBSERVER CORPS runs into Southampton Central with a service for Weymouth, 1962. *Jim Carter/Rail Photoprints Collection*

34050 ROYAL OBSERVER CORPS (21C150) entered service December 1946 coupled to a 4500 gallon/5 ton capacity tender. **R** August 1958. Withdrawn by BR August 1965 cut up at Birds Morriston, Swansea December 1965. **N**

The 1945 Royal Observer Corps Ensign. Note representation of the Imperial State Crown, from 1952 onwards the St Edward's Crown was used.

Royal Observer Corps was a civil defence organisation formed in 1925, whose civilian members were stood down in December 1995. The 'Corps' used optical devices to scan the skies for enemy aircraft, during the 'Battle' their 1000 plus members played a leading role in the nation's defence.

Rebuilt Bulleid 'Battle of Britain' Pacific BR No 34050 ROYAL OBSERVER CORPS is seen passing Basingstoke on 16 May 1964. Note the cabside adornment, the plaques in the colours of a long service medal ribbon (12 years), were mounted below the painted loco number on the cabsides. The plaques were unveiled on 2 July 1961 in a ceremony held at Waterloo station and carried out by Air Commodore C M Wight-Boycott, Commandant ROC. *David Anderson*

Rebuilt Bulleid 'Battle of Britain' Pacific BR No 34050 ROYAL OBSERVER CORPS is seen at Nine Elms depot (70A) in May 1960. Note the ex GWR Pannier tank behind it, an allocation indicative of that era.

The smartly turned out Rebuilt Bulleid 'Battle of Britain' Pacific BR No 34050 ROYAL OBSERVER CORPS is seen during a water stop at Westbury. The occasion was the Ian Allan 'Western Sunset' tour on 22 September 1962. Both images *Mike Morant Collection*

34051 WINSTON CHURCHILL (21C151) entered service December 1946 coupled to a 4500 gallon/5 ton capacity tender. Withdrawn by BR September 1965 for preservation as part of the National Collection (NRM). This was one of three engines named on 11 September 1947 at Waterloo station by Sir James Robb. **P**

The Right Honourable Sir Winston Leonard Spencer Churchill (1874–1965), the son of Lord Randolph Churchill and an American mother, was educated at Harrow and Sandhurst, becoming a soldier, politician and finally Britain's Prime Minister (serving two terms 1940–1945 and 1951–1955). Churchill fought with the British Army in India and Sudan, and as a journalist was captured in South Africa, from where his outstanding dispatches from the Boer War earned him public notice. Remembered for many things, not least of which his indomitable spirit, Winston Churchill was one of Britain's greatest 20th-century heroes. His bulldog like tenacity and steadfast refusal to make peace with Adolf Hitler made him the popular choice to lead Britain through World War II. Churchill is the only British Prime Minister to have won the Nobel Prize in Literature, and was the first person to be made an honorary citizen of the United States of America.

Churchill's funeral was the largest state funeral in world history up to that point in time, with representatives from 112 nations; only China did not send an emissary. By decree of the Queen, his body lay in state in Westminster Hall for three days thereafter a state funeral service was held at St Paul's Cathedral on 30 January 1965. One of the largest assemblages of statesmen in the world gathered for the service, which Queen Elizabeth II also attended. Churchill's lead-lined coffin passed up the River Thames from Tower Pier to Festival Pier on the MV *Havengore*, and as the funeral barge passed, London Dockers lowered their crane jibs in salute. The Royal Artillery fired the 19-gun salute due to a head of government, and the RAF staged a fly-by of 16 English Electric Lightning fighters. The coffin was then taken the short distance to Waterloo station where it was loaded onto a specially prepared and painted carriage as part of the funeral train for its rail journey to Hanborough, seven miles to the north-west of Oxford.

The funeral train, made up of Pullman coaches, was hauled by 'Battle of Britain' class locomotive No 34051 WINSTON CHURCHILL. Along the route taken by the train thousands of people stood in silence to pay their last respects. At Churchill's request, he was buried in the family plot at St Martin's Church, Bladon, near Woodstock. Churchill's funeral van, former Southern Railway Van No S2464S, is part of a preservation project at the Swanage Railway, Dorset.

Churchill had a hand in planning the details of his funeral service. Reportedly a senior BR/SR official suggested that Waterloo station was not the easiest one to facilitate the transfer of his cortege from river to train. Churchill reportedly fixed the official with a steely eye and replied 'If General de Gaulle dies before I do you can start the train from anywhere you like, but if I go first I go from Waterloo!'.

The funeral train seen between Goring & Streatley and Cholsey. *Hugh Ballantyne/ Rail Photoprints*

https://www.youtube.com/watch?v=X-NCn4Mxc_Y
Churchill's Funeral Train.

The Bulleid Light Pacific backs onto the train. *Keith Langston Collection*

Coat of Arms of Sir Winston Leonard Spencer-Churchill, KG, OM, CH, TD, PC, DL

On arrival of the cortege at Waterloo station the responsibility passed to the staff of British Railways (BR) in general and in particular to the Nine Elms depot engine crew, Driver Alf (Lou) Hurley, Fireman James (Jim) Lester and SR Chief Inspector Bill Neal. The Bulleid Light Pacific No 34051 had been specially prepared for the occasion. The Funeral Train consisted of five immaculate Pullman cars and a bogie van containing the coffin, all under the expert watchful eye of Royal Train Guard Mr WH Horwill.

In deference to the 'Great Man' three white SR/BR indicator discs style were used and accordingly fixed to represent the famous Churchillian 'V' for victory sign. At 13.28, with no whistle sounding, the train smoothly departed from Waterloo following a green flag from the guard. It was observed that members of the public stood heads bowed as the train passed by. All along the route uniformed ex-military personnel gave Sir Winston a last salute.

The three circular Southern Railway indicator discs in special formation on the locomotive's smokebox door are clearly visible as the train is pictured at speed near Didcot North Junction en route to Bladon. *David Anderson*

Preserved Bulleid Light Pacific BR No 34051 WINSTON CHURCHILL awaits departure from Bournemouth West with the Locomotive Club of Great Britain (LCGB) 'Wessex Downsman No 2' railtour for Waterloo, on 2 May 1965. The tour ran outward from Waterloo via the S&DR route and Bristol to Bournemouth West and on the inward leg was hauled by No 34051 from Bournemouth West to Waterloo via Basingstoke. *Rail Photoprints Collection*

https://www.youtube.com/watch?v=Srn_cBqyumc
No 34051 goes to the Great Dorset Steam Fair.

Bulleid Light Pacific BR No 34051 WINSTON CHURCHILL rounds the curve on the approach to Battledown Flyover with an up local service. *Rail Photoprints Collection*

Air Chief Marshal Hugh Caswall Tremenheere Dowding, 1st Baron Dowding GCB, GCVO, CMG, (24 April 1882–15 February 1970) was the commander of RAF Fighter Command during the Battle of Britain. In the immediate pre war period Hugh Dowding oversaw the introduction of Hurricane and Spitfire aircraft into the RAF. He was amongst the first military commanders to recognise the great value of RADAR and he oversaw its implementation and successful use (in conjunction with the Royal Observer Corps). Lord Dowding's son Derek was a pilot with 74 Squadron.

Hugh Caswall Tremenheere Dowding served as a fighter pilot and then as commanding officer of No 16 Squadron for the duration of World War II. During the inter-war years, he became Air Officer Commanding Fighting Area, Air Defence of Great Britain, and thereafter joined the Air Council as Air Member for Supply and Research. He was RAF Fighter Command's 'Air Officer Commanding' during the Battle of Britain, and is generally credited with playing a crucial role in Britain's defence, and hence, the defeat of Adolf Hitler's plan to invade Britain. *Royal Air Force*

Rebuilt Bulleid Light Pacific BR No 34052 LORD DOWDING is seen preparing to leave Basingstoke. The Bulleid Firth Brown (BFB) steel wheels are shown to good effect in this image. The original American so called Boxpok wheels are similar in appearance but are of a fabricated design, whilst the SR/BR BFB wheels are cast as 'one piece' units. *David Anderson*

Rebuilt Bulleid Light Pacific BR No 34052 LORD DOWDING is seen passing Eastleigh with an infrastructure train (ballast) in November 1966. Note that the locomotive's nameplate and crest have been removed. *Keith Langston Collection*

Rebuilt Bulleid Light Pacific BR No 34052 LORD DOWDING is seen at the north end of Bincombe tunnel. No 34052 is in charge of a van train known as one of the 'Weymouth Special 17' and as such was the second of 3 such specials which ran on the final day of steam on the BR/SR Sunday July 9 1967. All three specials were bound for Bescot and they were steam hauled as far as Westbury. *Mike Morant Collection*

Newly restored Rebuilt 'Battle of Britain' Light Pacific BR No 34053 SIR KEITH PARK enters Kidderminster station, Severn Valley Railway with a service from Bridgnorth as the signalman looks on admiringly, 17 July 2015. *John Chalcraft/Rail Photoprints*

BEWARE
OF
TRAINS

34053 SIR KEITH PARK (21C153) entered SR service January 1947 coupled to a 4500 gallon/5 ton capacity tender. **R** November 1958, withdrawn by BR October 1965 and rescued from the scrapyard of Woodham Brothers, Barry for preservation. This was one of three engines named on 19 September at Brighton station, when Air Chief Marshal Park actually named his own engine. **P. N.**

Air Chief Marshal Sir Keith Rodney Park GCB, KBE, MC & bar, DFC, RAF (15 June 1892–6 February 1975) hailed from New Zealand. Keith Park was a First World War flying ace. In April 1940 Park took command of No 11 Group RAF, and was responsible for the fighter defence of London and southeast England. He also organized fighter patrols over France during the Dunkirk evacuation and in the Battle of Britain his command took the brunt of the Luftwaffe's air attacks. Park flew his personal Hurricane around his fighter airfields during the battle and was a popular hands-on commander. The Germans rightly called him 'Defender of London'.

https://www.youtube.com/watch?v=FmtMRJ_eYKo
BR No 34053 SIR KEITH PARK, in action on the Severn Valley Railway 2014.

Royal Air Force, Air Vice-Marshal (later Air Chief Marshal) Sir Keith Park is seen in front of his Hurricane (call sign 'OK-2') on the George Cross Island of Malta. *Royal Air Force*

The immaculately restored rebuilt 'Battle of Britain class' Light Pacific BR No 34053 SIR KEITH PARK is seen facing the buffer stops at Kidderminster station, Severn Valley Railway at the time of a special rededication ceremony which was held in August 2013. The locomotive is owned by Southern Locomotives Limited. *Keith Langston*

34054 LORD BEAVERBROOK (21C154) entered SR service January 1947 coupled to a 4500 gallon/5 ton capacity tender. Withdrawn by BR September 1964 cut up at Birds, Bynea March 1965. This was one of three engines named at Waterloo station on 16 September 1947.

William Maxwell 'Max' Aitken, 1st Baron Beaverbrook, Bt, PC, (25 May 1879–9 June 1964) was a Canadian-British business tycoon, politician, and writer. Max Aitken was a close friend of Churchill who initially appointed him as Minister of Aircraft Production; he later became Minister of Supply. His son Max Aitken Jr. was a fighter pilot with 601 Squadron.

Bulleid Light Pacific BR No 34054 LORD BEAVERBROOK stands at Exeter St. Davids station with a mixed passenger service, conveying coaching stock and a pair of 6-wheel milk tanks, during April 1964. *Hugh Ballantyne/Rail Photoprints*

Bulleid Light Pacific BR No 34054 LORD BEAVERBROOK is seen backing onto a service for the West of England at London Waterloo station. *David Anderson*

34055 FIGHTER PILOT (21C155) entered SR service February 1947 coupled to a 4500 gallon/5 ton capacity tender. Withdrawn by BR June 1963 cut up at Eastleigh Works May 1964.

This loco was named in honour of the fighter pilots who took part in the Battle of Britain, the naming ceremony being performed on 19 September 1947 at Brighton Station by Group Captain Douglas Bader.

The so called Bulleid Southern Railway numbers were an adaptation of the International Union of Railways (UIC) classification system (also known as the German system) of using letters and numbers to designate the powered and unpowered axles, together with a running number. Thus the 'BB' class 4-6-2 locomotives became 21C1 – where '2' and '1'refer to the number of unpowered leading and trailing axles respectively, and 'C' refers to the number of driving axles (in this case 3). The numbers following the 'C' prefix refer to the locomotive's running (stock) number.

Bulleid Light Pacific BR No 34055 FIGHTER PILOT is seen at Bricklayers Arms depot (73B) in 1961. *Martyn Hunt/Rail Photoprints Collection*

This image of Bulleid Light Pacific SR No 21C155 (then running un-named) between Bromley South and Shortlands with a Ramsgate–London Victoria service in 1947, clearly shows the Bulleid numbering system. *Dave Cobbe-C.R.L. Coles Collection/Rail Photoprints*

34056 CROYDON (21C156) entered SR service February 1947 coupled to a 4500 gallon/5 ton capacity tender. R December 1960. Withdrawn by BR May 1967 cut up at John Cashmore, Newport September 1967.

Considered to be the world's first international airfield Croydon (Croydon is designated a London Borough but is historically part of Surrey). The airfield was extensively used for commercial flying throughout the 1920s and 1930s. The RAF took over the site at the onset of WWII and it was used as a satellite field to Kenley. It was badly damaged in August 1940 when German bombers mistook it for Kenley. Croydon Airport closed in the 1950s.

Bulleid Light Pacific BR No 34056 CROYDON is seen in original form at Yeovil Junction whilst waiting to head a down LSWR route service on 19 September 1959. *Rail Photoprints Collection*

Bulleid Light Pacific BR No 34056 CROYDON is seen in re-built form whilst leaving Exeter Central with an eastbound service, in April 1964. *Rail Photoprints Collection*

Bullied Light Pacific BR No 34056 CROYDON is seen at Plymouth Friary shed (72D), in July 1956. Note that the air smoothed casing is in a poor condition. *Dave Cobbe Collection/Rail Photoprints*

Bullied Light Pacific BR No 34056 CROYDON is seen on shed at Yeovil (72C) in August 1959, a year prior to being rebuilt. *Mike Morant Collection*

This image shows to good effect the front end design of the casing, where the roof has been extended incorporating a slot. That design, in conjunction with the side smoke deflectors, was an attempt to overcome smoke drift problems which could impede the driver's forward view. Reportedly these modifications helped but did not completely solve the problems.

34057 BIGGIN HILL (21C157) entered SR service March 1947 coupled to a 4500 gallon/5 ton capacity tender. Withdrawn by BR May 1967 and cut up by John Cashmore, Newport October 1967.

Biggin Hill Airport was opened during the First World War initially for wireless experiments but later as a home for 141 Squadron in the defence of London. Between the wars it was used for development work on instrument design, anti-aircraft devices and night flying. During WWII Biggin Hill was a command base for the 'Battle of Britain' and home to squadrons of Spitfires and Hurricanes, its importance was such that between August 1940 and January 1941 it was targeted 12 times by the Luftwaffe, but it was never put out of action. After the war it remained in military use until 1974 when it was sold to the London Borough of Bromley and today it is home to private aviation service facilities and regularly used for business and corporate flights.

Bulleid Light Pacific BR No 34057 BIGGIN HILL had almost come to the end of its working life when this picture was taken at Nine Elms depot (70A) in April 1967. Note that the smokebox number plate has been removed and replaced by a temporary one and that the nameplates/crests and shed plate have also been removed. The location of a battery, under a cover/step on the front buffer beam, can also be seen. *Keith Langston Collection*

On the last weekend of service on the Somerset and Dorset Bulleid Light Pacifics BR Nos 34006 BUDE ('WC' class) and 34057 BIGGIN HILL head south over Tucking Mill Viaduct with the LCGB's 'Somerset and Dorset Railtour' on Saturday 5 March 1966. *Hugh Ballantyne/Rail Photoprints*

Evercreech Junction on 5 March 1966. Battle of Britain Light Pacific BR No 34057 BIGGIN HILL awaits the arrival of the LCGB's 'Somerset and Dorset' railtour which it will double-head from Evercreech to Bath Green Park with 'WC' class BR No 34006 BUDE. *Hugh Ballantyne/Rail Photoprints*

34058 SIR FREDERICK PILE (21C158) entered SR service April 1947 coupled to a 4500 gallon/5 ton capacity tender, this locomotive was temporarily converted for oil burning in 1947. **R** November 1960. When named Southern Railway mistakenly placed Sir Frederick Pile's coat of arms on KENLEY and the RAF badge intended for that locomotive on SIR FREDERICK PILE. British Railways never corrected that mistake. Withdrawn by BR October 1964 sent for scrapping to Woodham Bros, Barry but later rescued for preservation. **P**

General Sir Frederick Alfred Pile, 2nd Baronet GCB DSO MC (14 September 1884–14 November 1976) served in both World Wars. The Dublin born officer was General Officer Commanding of Anti-Aircraft Command during the WWII. Frederick Pile became Director General of Housing with the Ministry of Works under the post war government.

Two images of Rebuilt Bulleid Light Pacific BR No 34058 SIR FREDERICK PILE. The Light Pacific is seen in September 1963 'on shed' at Weymouth (original BR shed code 82F, changed to 71G in 1958, and in September 1963 it changed again to 70G). *Rail Photoprints Collection*

The engine is seen passing through Vauxhall in September 1964. The locomotive is in a very grimy condition with the nameplates having already been removed, although the backing plates are still in place. This preserved locomotive is privately owned. *Keith Langston Collection*

34059 SIR ARCHIBALD SINCLAIR (21C159) entered SR service April 1947 coupled to a 4500 gallon/5 ton capacity tender. **R** March 1960. Withdrawn by BR May 1966 sent for scrapping to Woodham Bros, Barry but later rescued for preservation. **P**

Archibald Henry Macdonald Sinclair, 1st Viscount Thurso KT, CMG, PC (22th October 1890–15 June 1970), known as Sir Archibald Sinclair, Bt between 1912 and 1952, and often referred to as Archie Sinclair. He was a Scottish politician and one-time leader of the British Liberal Party. In 1940 'Archie Sinclair' became Secretary of State for Air in Churchill's wartime coalition government.

Bulleid Light Pacific BR No 34059 SIR ARCHIBALD SINCLAIR is seen passing Woking in the summer of 1959. *Keith Langston Collection*

Rebuilt Bulleid Light Pacific BR No 34059 SIR ARCHIBALD SINCLAIR is seen on the down through road as it approaches Seaton Junction with a down West of England express, summer, 1964. *David Anderson*

Rebuilt Bulleid Light Pacific BR No 34059 SIR ARCHIBALD SINCLAIR is seen as a preserved locomotive, whilst hard at work on the Bluebell Railway. The locomotive is owned by the Bulleid Society. *Paul Pettitt*

Two more glorious images of Rebuilt Bulleid Light Pacific BR No 34059 SIR ARCHIBALD SINCLAIR hard at work on the Bluebell Railway, taken in October 2009.
Paul Pettitt

34060 25 SQUADRON (21C160) entered SR service April 1947 coupled to a 4500 gallon/5 ton capacity tender. **R** November 1960. Withdrawn by BR June 1967 cut up by John Cashmore, Newport April–September 1968.

25 Squadron was primarily a night fighter squadron.

Aircraft: Bristol Blenheim Mk.1F and Bristol Beaufighter Mk. 1F.
Motto: Feriens tego 'Striking I defend'.
Stations operated from, Martlesham Heath 19 June 1940, North Weald
1 September 1940 and Debden 8 October 1940.

The design is a hawk rising afrontée on a gauntlet. This badge was approved for the squadron's use by HM King Edward VIII in October 1936.

Rebuilt Bulleid Light Pacific BR No 34060 25 SQUADRON is seen with a down train at Seaton Junction in 1963. Seaton Junction was a popular location with steam photographers, it is situated on the ex L&SWR main line now the West of England mainline and is approximately 3 miles west of Axminster. The station and branch line were both closed in March, 1966 following the drop in holiday rail passengers after the increase in car travel. *David Anderson*

Rebuilt Bulleid Light Pacific BR No 34060 25 SQUADRON is seen in the company of West Country class Light Pacific BR No 34013 OAKHAMPTON at Eastleigh in June 1965.

Note from the above image that electric lighting was provided on the locomotive. Footplate lighting was also a design feature; the power was provided by a steam generator which was located below the footplate (during later modifications back up batteries were added). The gauges were lit by ultra-violet light thus enabling clearer night time vision of the boiler steam pressure gauge and the brake pipe vacuum pressure gauge whilst reportedly eliminating dazzle, and making life easier for the crew. The cab was designed using ergonomic principles, with the main operating controls being grouped according to the needs of both driver and fireman. As an aid to the fireman, a foot treadle using steam pressure to open the firehole doors was incorporated in the design. Additionally, the footplate was entirely enclosed, in order to improve locomotive crew working conditions during winter.

34061 73 SQUADRON (21C161) entered SR service April 1940 coupled to a 4500 gallon/5 ton capacity tender. Withdrawn by BR August 1964 cut up by Woods, Queenborough March 1965.

73 Squadron was a unit with night fighting capabilities. It was one of two squadrons operated in France as part of the Advanced Air Striking Force (AASF) it returned to England on 18 June 1940.

Aircraft: Hawker Hurricane Mk.1.
Motto: Tutor et ultor – 'Protector and avenger'.
Stations operated from, Church Fenton 18 June 1940 and Castle Camps 5 September 1940.

This official badge design is in the form of a demi-talbot rampant, which is charged with a maple leaf on the shoulder. During World War Two the squadron was commanded by a Major Hubbard and his aircraft carried a representation of Old Mother Hubbard's dog looking into an empty cupboard. In order to retain its association with this unofficial badge the squadron adopted a heraldic dog and put a maple leaf on it to mark its association with Canadian personnel.

Bulleid Light Pacific BR No 34061 73 SQUADRON is seen at Exmouth Junction Depot (72A changed to BR/WR 83D in 1963) the locomotive is in the company of sister Bulleid Light Pacific BR No 34060 25 SQUADRON, June 1955. *David Anderson*

Bulleid Light Pacific BR No 34061 73 SQUADRON is seen near Basingstoke circa 1963, note the damage (crease) to the air smoothed casing. *David Anderson*

Rebuilt Bulleid Light Pacific BR No 34062 17 SQUADRON prepares to leave Waterloo with the 17.00 service to Yeovil Town, on 8 June 1963. Note the wooden planks serving as safety guards against the electrified 3rd rail. *Ian Turnbull/Rail Photoprints*

34062 17 SQUADRON (21C162) entered SR service May 1947 coupled to a 4500 gallon/5 ton capacity tender. R April 1959. Withdrawn by BR August 1964 cut up by Birds, Bridgend between June 1965 and June 1966.

17 Squadron was used to cover the retreat of allied troops from Europe. The squadron also operated from Brittany before returning to the UK via the Channel Islands. The squadron operated over Southern England during the whole of the 'Battle'.

Aircraft: Hurricane Mk.1.
Motto: Excellere contende – 'Strive to excel'.
Stations operated from, Debden 19 June 1940, Tangmere 19 August 1940, Debden 2 September 1940 and Martlesham Heath 8 October 1940.

The badge design includes an armoured medieval gauntlet, thus symbolizing armed strength. The gauntlet also celebrates the fact that the squadron previously operated the single seat bi-plane Gloster Gauntlet fighter aircraft in the 1930s.

Bulleid Light Pacific BR No 34062 17 SQUADRON is seen approaching Honiton with a down service, circa 1950. Honiton station was opened by the London and South Western Railway (LSWR) in 1860 and in modern times it is a stopping place on the London Waterloo to Exeter route. Note how during the steam era the lineside foliage was cut down to a low level (mainly during spring and summer) in order to reduce the chance of lineside fires. *Rail Photoprints Collection*

229 Squadron was originally formed in August 1918 then disbanded in December 1919 and reformed in October 1939. In May 1940 229 sent one of its flights to operate out of France for 8 days and then after flying defensive patrols over the east coast the squadron moved to Essex in September 1940, and remained there for the whole of the 'Battle'.

Aircraft: Hurricane Mk.1.
Motto: 'Be bold'.
Stations operated from, Wittering 26 June 1940 and Northolt 9 September 1940. (It became No. 603 Squadron RAF in January 1945).

The badge design includes a boar's head pierced by a sword. The badge represents triumph over a powerful and ferocious enemy.

Bulleid Light Pacific BR No 34063 229 SQUADRON is seen at Nine Elms (70A), circa 1956. Nine Elms locomotive works were built in 1839 by the London and South Western Railway (LSWR) adjoining their passenger terminus near the Vauxhall end of Nine Elms Lane, in the London Borough of Battersea. They were rebuilt in 1841 and remained the principal locomotive carriage and wagon workshops of that railway until closure in stages between 1891 and 1909. Thereafter a large motive power depot remained open on the site until 1967, serving Waterloo station. *Rail Photoprints Collection*

Bulleid Light Pacific BR No 34063 229 SQUADRON is seen in the afternoon sun at Nine Elms depot (70A) in August 1963. The locomotive was at that time allocated to Brighton and it is thought that this image was taken following a 'running in turn' after the engine had spent a period in Brighton Works. No 34063 was allocated to Salisbury (70E at that time, formerly 72B) in the September of that year. *Mike Morant Collection*

A view of the Battle of Britain Operations Room at Fighter Command's 'No 10 Group HQ' at RAF Box, Rudloe Manor, Wiltshire. Women's Auxiliary Air Force (WAAF) plotters can be seen at work under the watchful eyes of the duty officers.

'We had not flinched or wavered … The soul of the British people … had proved invincible.
We had shown the world that we could hold our own.'
Winston S. Churchill 1940

https://www.youtube.com/watch?v=52YOKT_O10U
The Battle of Britain.

34064 FIGHTER COMMAND (21C164) entered SR service July 1947 coupled to a 4500 gallon/5 ton capacity tender. This was the 1000th locomotive built at Brighton works. Named at Waterloo station on 11 September 1947 by Sir James Robb. Withdrawn by BR May 1966 cut up by Birds, Bridgend November 1966. **N**

Above: The locomotive carried a crest depicting the famous RAF Per Ardua Ad Astra – *Through Adversity to the Stars* motto.

Right: At an Air Council meeting on 1 August 1918, a badge for adoption by the Royal Air Force was approved. The badge adopted was similar in design to the one shown with the exception that the circlet surrounding the eagle then comprised a garter and a buckle.

Post 1951 Crest.

Fighter Command was formed in 1936. The command was divided into a number of 'Groups', each controlling specific areas of Britain. During the 'Battle' 11 Group, which controlled South East England and London, took the full force of the Luftwaffe attacks. Other groups included 10 Group which covered South West England, 12 Group which covered the Midlands and East Anglia and 13 Group which covered the North of England and Scotland.

Bulleid Light Pacific BR No 34064 FIGHTER COMMAND is seen L/E near Staines circa 1965. In January No 34064 was chosen as the standby engine for Churchill's funeral train. *Mike Morant Collection*

Not a common sight in East Wales, Bulleid Light Pacific BR No 34064 FIGHTER COMMAND is seen at Ruabon with the 'Talyllyn Special' a 2-day charter train, on 28/29 September 1963. In total three locomotives were used with No 34064 taking charge of the outward leg from London Paddington to Ruabon on 28 and the return leg from Shrewsbury to Paddington on 29. *R. A. Whitfield/Rail Photoprints Collection*

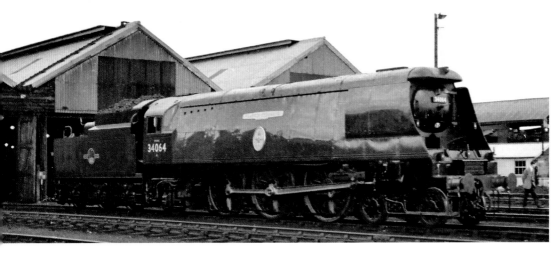

Bulleid Light Pacific BR No 34064 FIGHTER COMMAND is seen in ex works condition at Eastleigh depot (71A). Note the side view of the oblong Giesl ejector (in the normal chimney position). The ejector unit was fitted in April 1962 and No 34064 was the only member of the 'BB' class to receive that modification. *Mike Morant Collection*

A Giesl ejector is a suction draught system for steam locomotives. This ejector was invented in 1951 by the Austrian engineer, Dr. Adolph Giesl-Gieslingen. The ejector improved suction draught resulting in a correspondingly better use of energy. The existing blastpipe in a locomotive is replaced by several, small, fan-shaped, diverging blast pipes, from which the diffuser gets its flat, long, drawn-out shape. In use the ejector fitted to No 34064 was regarded as an improvement and as a consequence the locomotive was held in high regard by BR/SR locomotive crews.

The Giesl Ejector from the Talyllyn Railway narrow gauge locomotive No 4 is seen on display at the Narrow Gauge Railway Museum, Tywyn. *Keith Langston Collection*

Hawker Hurricane

Hawker employees Winnie Bennett, Dolly Bennett, Florence Simpson and a colleague at work on the production of *Hurricane* fighter aircraft at a factory in Britain, in 1942.
Imperial War Museum

The Hurricane was ordered into production in June 1936, mainly due to its relatively simple construction and ease of manufacture. As war was looking increasingly likely, and time was of the essence in providing the RAF with an effective fighter aircraft, it was unclear if the more advanced Spitfire would enter production smoothly, while the Hurricane used well-understood manufacturing techniques. The first 50 Hurricanes had reached squadrons by the middle of 1938.

At that time, production was slightly greater than the RAF's capacity to introduce the new aircraft and the government gave Hawkers the clearance to sell the excess to nations likely to oppose German expansion. As a result, there were some modest sales to other countries.

By the time of the German invasion of Poland (September 1939), there were 18 operational Hurricane squadrons and three more were in the process of converting.

Preserved Hurricane Mk1, RAF serial R4118, Squadron code UP-W, UK civil registration G-HUPW, made an evocotive sight when seen at the Royal International Air Tattoo, Fairford, Gloucestershire, in 2008. *Adrian Pingstone*

The Hawker Hurricane was the first operational RAF aircraft capable of top speeds in excess of 300 mph, powered by one 1030 hp Rolls Royce Merlin 12-cylinder engine it was designed by Sydney Camm. A total of 1,715 Hurricanes flew in the 'Battle', a larger number than the additional total of all the other fighters combined. It was thought of as a 'go anywhere do anything fighter' and although an older design than the Spitfire its pilots were nevertheless credited with four-fifths of all enemy aircraft destroyed between July and October 1940.

Wartime colour photo of Hurricane IIC *BE500* flown by Squadron Leader Denis Smallwood of 87 Squadron in the RDM2 ("Special Night") scheme and used on intruder operations 1941–1942. *Royal Air Force*

34065 HURRICANE (21C165) entered SR service July 1947 coupled to a 4500 gallon/5 ton capacity tender. This was one of three engines named at Waterloo station on 16 September 1947. The other locomotives were No 34054 **LORD BEAVERBROOK** and No 34066 **SPITFIRE**. Withdrawn by BR April 1964 and cut up by Birds, Morriston November 1964. **N**

See also GWR/BRWR chapter entry for locomotive No 5072.

Bulleid Light Pacific BR No 34065 HURRICANE is seen in light steam and with a full tender of coal at Exmouth Junction (then 83D) whilst in the company of a sister Light Pacific, during the spring of 1962. The loco at that time rightly carried a (72A) Stewarts Lane depot shedplate and that location was re-coded (75D) in June 1962. *Rail Photoprints Collection*

Bulleid Light Pacific BR No 34065 HURRICANE is seen approaching Basingstoke with a down express, circa 1963. *David Anderson*

Preserved WWII 'Spitfire' LF Mk IX is seen whilst being flown by Ray Hanna during an air display. This venerable aircraft is credited with shooting down a German Focke – Wulf '190', during 1943, whilst serving with '222 Squadron'. Squadron Leader Raynham George Hanna AFC with bar, (28/08/1928–01/12/2005) was a New Zealand-born pilot who served with the Royal Air Force. During his time in the RAF, he was a founding member of the Red Arrows display team. *Franck Cabrol*

The Supermarine Spitfire was designed by R.G. Mitchell and the prototype first flew in 1936. The first production versions powered by a 1,030 hp Rolls Royce Merlin III twelve-cylinder engine entered RAF service between August and December 1938, top speed 362 mph. At the start of the battle 19 squadrons were fully operational with the type. A total of 1,583 Spitfire Mk1s were built and they were followed by the Mk 11 version which was fitted with a 1,175-h.p. Rolls Royce Merlin XII engine. However, it was the Mk1 which bore the brunt of the fighting during the 'Battle'. The Spitfire is undoubtedly one of the most famous aircraft ever built.

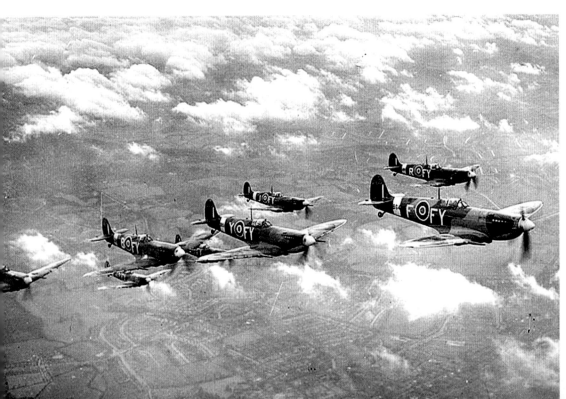

A superb image of 8 early 'Mark IXBs' Spitfires of 611 Squadron which was based at Biggin Hill in late 1942. 611 Squadron was not one of those chosen for a locomotive name. *Royal Air Force*

125

34066 SPITFIRE (21C166) entered SR service September 1947 coupled to a 4500 gallon/5 ton capacity tender. This was one of three engines named at Waterloo station on 16 September 1947. Withdrawn by BR September 1966 cut up by J. Buttigieg, Newport January 1967. **N**

See also GWR/BRWR chapter entry for locomotive No 5071.

Bulleid Light Pacific BR No 34066 SPITFIRE is seen at Ramsgate in 1955, the headcode and Pullman coach suggests it could be working one of the several 'Man of Kent' services. *Rail Photoprints Collection*

Bulleid Light Pacific BR No 34066 SPITFIRE is seen under the coaling stage at Nine Elms depot (70A), circa 1965. *Mike Morant Collection*

Bulleid Light Pacific BR No 34066 SPITFIRE is seen at Tunbridge Wells West with the RCTS/LCGB 'Sussex Downsman' Railtour from Waterloo, on 22 March 1964. *Hugh Ballantyne/Rail Photoprints Collection*

Bulleid Light Pacific BR No 34066 SPITFIRE is once again seen at Tunbridge Wells West with the RCTS/LCGB 'Sussex Downsman' Railtour. *Mike Morant Collection*

Sadly, 'BB' class BR No 34066 SPITFIRE was involved in the disastrous Lewisham Rail Crash, which occurred on 4 December 1957 (just outside St. Johns station). The train hauled by No 34066 reportedly passed two yellow caution signals in foggy conditions and as a result collided with a stationary train, 90 people lost their lives and 173 were injured. The enquiry concluded that restricted visibility from the unrebuilt Light Pacific locomotive cabs was a contributory factor. Thereafter all the Bulleid Light Pacifics were gradually fitted with Automatic Warning System (AWS) equipment. No 34066 was later repaired by BR and put back into service.

A delightful scene at Barnstaple in 'Glorious Devon' as Bulleid Light Pacific BR No 34066 SPITFIRE is seen crossing the River Taw with a service from Ilfracombe, on 16 June 1962. Note the painted CND symbols, indicative of the period. *Dave Cobbe/Rail Photoprints Collection*

34067 TANGMERE (21C167) entered SR service September 1947 coupled to a 4500 gallon/5 ton capacity tender. The locomotive was named at Brighton station on 19 September 1947. Three 'BB' class locomotives were named on that occasion, the other two being **SIR KEITH PARK** and **FIGHTER PILOT**. The RAF officers conducting the ceremonies were Air Chief Marshall Sir Keith Park, Group Captain D.R.S. Bader and Wing Commander W.G. Clouston. Withdrawn by BR November 1963 and sent to Woodham Bros Barry scrapyard for cutting up, but was rescued from there for preservation in January 1981. **P**

RAF Tangmere was a famous Battle of Britain Royal Air Force station located approximately 3 miles east of Chichester in West Sussex. On 16 August Tangmere was all but destroyed during an attack by German Junkers 88 Stuka dive bombers, hangers, living accommodation and workshops were destroyed and most of the station's infrastructure wrecked. However, despite the severe damage and number of casualties the airfield remained operational.

https://www.youtube.com/watch?v=WZCSxlmIdeA
Tangmere THE WELSHMAN Poole to Cardiff.

Preserved 'Battle of Britain' class Bulleid Light Pacific BR No 34067 TANGMERE is seen in full cry! Complete with 'Golden Arrow' embellishments the locomotive is seen approaching Frant station Kent with the 'Battle of Hastings' tour which took place on 8 July 2006 the locomotive was operated by the West Coast Railway Company. *Paul Pettitt*

Preserved Bulleid Light Pacific BR No 34067 TANGMERE is seen at Woodham's scrapyard Barry, South Wales prior to being rescued. After rescue the engine was stored for a long period prior to being rebuilt at the works of Riley & Son, Bury, Lancashire. *Keith Langston Collection*

Bulleid Light Pacific BR No 34067 TANGMERE is seen at Basingstoke during April 1962. Almost all of the 'BB' class locomotives carried the appropriate device or squadron badges. In addition to an RAF badge TANGMERE carried station badges donated by the sergeants' mess and fixed on the cabsides. *Rail Photoprints Collection*

Preserved Bulleid Light Pacific BR No 34067 TANGMERE is seen crossing the river Adur near Ford, West Sussex during September 2006. *Paul Pettitt*

Preserved Bulleid Light Pacific BR No 34067 TANGMERE is seen early in its preserved life whilst climbing Burrs on the East Lancashire Railway, during March 2003. *Fred Kerr*

34068 KENLEY (21C168) entered SR service October 1947 coupled to a 4500 gallon/5 ton capacity tender. When named Southern Railway mistakenly placed Sir Frederick Pile's coat of arms on **KENLEY** and the RAF badge intended for that locomotive on **SIR FREDERICK PILE**. British Railways never corrected that mistake. Withdrawn by BR December 1963 cut up by BR Eastleigh Works March 1964.

Kenley Motto: NISI DOMINUS PRO NOBIS – *We depend on the Lord.*

Located just to the west of Biggin Hill, RAF Kenley suffered its worst damage in an attack on 18 August 1940. All ten hangars and twelve aircraft, including ten Hurricanes were destroyed, and the runways badly cratered, there were many casualties. During the attacks the Sector Operations Room had to be moved to an emergency location away from the airfield. Together with Biggin Hill and Croydon, Kenley was responsible for the air defence of London.

In the modern era the field is in use as a Glider flying/training facility and is known as 'The Surrey Hills Gliding Club'.

The aerodrome was used as a location for films which included *Angels One Five* (1952) and *Reach for the Sky* (1956), the latter about Douglas Bader who was posted to RAF Kenley in 1930 No. 23 Squadron RAF shortly before his accident in 1931.

A few of the buildings survive, although the control tower was demolished after a fire in 1978 along with the remaining hangars. Even so Kenley is thought to be the best preserved of all Second World War RAF fighter stations, with the runway still in its original configuration. English Heritage (in 2000) identified Kenley as 'The most complete fighter airfield associated with the Battle of Britain to have survived'. The respective councils of Croydon and Tandridge have designated the airfield site as a Conservation Area (2006).

Bulleid Light Pacific BR No 34068 KENLEY is seen on shed at Exmouth Junction (72A) in August 1963. The locomotive has a full tender of coal and has been serviced in anticipation of its next rostered turn. *Rail Photoprints Collection*

34069 HAWKINGE (21C169) entered SR service October 1947 coupled to a 4500 gallon/5 ton capacity tender. Withdrawn by BR November 1963 and cut up at BR Eastleigh Works May 1964.

Hawkinge, Kent is situated about 3 miles from Folkestone and was often referred to by RAF personnel as 'Hell Fire Corner' as it was under the direct flight path of German bombers out of the Pas de Calais region of France, making for targets in London and the south of England. Although most of the old airfield has since been built upon, a single hanger remains, and that authentic building houses the impressive 'Kent Battle of Britain Museum'.

It was from Hawkinge that air liaison was maintained between the Royal Air Force and the British Expeditionary Force during the fighting in France and the Dunkirk evacuation in 1940. As long as communications remained open, targets were selected in accordance with requests from the BEF and Hawkinge was one of the advanced re-fuelling bases when maximum range was required for operations over France. It was a fighter airfield for squadrons of No. 11 Group, and was so severely damaged by German bombing and machine gun attacks during the Battle of Britain that it had to be abandoned temporarily.

The very grimy looking Bulleid Light Pacific BR No 34069 HAWKINGE is seen approaching Basingstoke with an up West of England express, in May 1962. *Rail Photoprints Collection*

Bulleid Light Pacific BR No 34069 HAWKINGE climbs away from Shortlands, apparently with steam to spare, whilst hauling a 'Kentish Belle' Pullman service on 19 August 1951. 'The Kentish Belle' (also 'Kentish Belle') London Victoria–Ramsgate was a summer only Pullman service that first ran on 2 July 1951(also served Canterbury in 1951 only). The last titled run of this train was on 14 September 1958. *Mike Morant Collection*

34070 MANSTON (21C170) entered SR service October 1947 coupled to a 4500 gallon/5 ton capacity tender. Withdrawn by BR August 1964 and sent to Woodham Bros, Barry scrapyard for cutting up, but was rescued from there for preservation in June 1983. **P**

Manston airfield is in the north east corner of Kent and being equipped with one long and very wide runway it was used as an emergency landing airfield for bomber aircraft that were in distress. For the duration of the Battle of Britain Manston became a fighter aircraft base and as such was heavily bombed by the Luftwaffe. As a consequence, its buildings and infrastructure suffered great damage. In modern times the facility has become Kent International Airport. In addition, there are three appropriate museums on the site.

Below: Now Preserved Bulleid Light Pacific BR No 34070 MANSTON. Above, No 34070 is seen at Woodham Bros, Barry scrapyard in 1966 prior to being rescued for restoration by the Manston Locomotive Preservation Society (1983). *John Chalcraft/Rail Photoprints Collection*

Bottom: The locomotive is seen at Corfe Castle on the Swanage Railway, No 34070 is in the care of Southern Locomotives Limited. *David Gibson*

Preserved Bulleid Light Pacific BR No 34070 MANSTON is seen in the evening light, at Swanage station after a heavy rain shower. *Fred Kerr*

MANSTON again seen at work on the Swanage Railway, March 2010. *David Gibson*

Note the Southern Railway 'Route Indicator Discs' on two of the eight front end lamp brackets. By arranging the discs on differing brackets a specific route code could be created. The codes were intended for the use of railway staff in general, and signallers in particular. The SR codes were displayed by discs during daylight hours and lamps during darkness. In modern times the discs and lamps were almost always white. The flat metal discs have a hook fixed to the top of them facilitating attachment to the locomotives' lamp brackets.

Preserved Bulleid Light Pacific BR No 34070 MANSTON gets smartly away from Corfe Castle on the Swanage Railway. The RAF badge is on the crest carried by the locomotive. *Paul Pettitt*

Two more delightful images of Preserved Bulleid Light Pacific BR No 34070 MANSTON at work on the Swanage Railway during 2009. *Paul Pettitt*

https://www.youtube.com/watch?v=TkX3qw2EfZw
Battle of Britain locomotives at the Swanage Railway.

34071 601 SQUADRON entered BR service April 1948 coupled to a 5500 gallon/5 ton capacity tender. When first introduced No 34071 carried the name **615 SQUADRON** for a short while during 1948 (that name later given to No 34082). **R** May 1960. Withdrawn by BR April 1967 cut up by John Cashmore, Newport September 1967.

601 Squadron was known as the County of London Squadron. During the German invasion of France, the squadron operated for a week from French soil, after which it was based in England for the duration of the 'Battle'.

Aircraft: Hawker Hurricane Mk.1.
Stations operated from Tangmere 17 June 1940, Debden 19 August 1940, Tangmere 2 September 1940, and Exeter 7 September 1940.

Below: Bulleid Light Pacific BR No 34071 601 SQUADRON is seen with a 'Golden Arrow' working at Folkestone Warren in 1953, note early BR crest. *Rail Photoprints Collection*

Bottom: Bulleid Light Pacific BR No 34071 601 SQUADRON in 'Rebuilt' form is seen at Eastleigh depot (71A) in July 1960, note late BR crest. *Rail Photoprints Collection*

'The Golden Arrow' – Flèche d'Or', London Victoria–Dover (Marine) for Calais and Paris (Nord) was a Pullman car service which first ran on 15 May 1929. The title was discontinued on 3 September 1939 and reinstated on 15 April 1946. The service continued after the end of steam on BR and its last titled run took place on 30 September 1972.

https://www.youtube.com/watch?v=JF0kMPoU-1A
'The Golden Arrow' in colour, a 1949 film.

Bulleid Light Pacific BR No 34071 601 SQUADRON is seen in BR Malachite livery at Brighton circa 1948. When ex-works in April 1948 BR No 34071 was named 615 SQUADRON, and then subsequently renamed 601 SQUADRON on 16 September 1948 at Brighton Station, reportedly by Sir Malcolm Fraser. That was the last Battle of Britain class official naming ceremony, other locomotives simply leaving the works with their nameplates and crests attached. *Mike Morant Collection*

Bulleid Light Pacific BR No 34071 601 SQUADRON hurries through Bromley at the head of a down 'Golden Arrow' service, circa 1955. *Rail Photoprints Collection*

https://www.youtube.com/watch?v=hPE9VbuUq_w
Golden Arrow recreation with 'Tangmere'.

Rebuilt Bulleid Light Pacific BR No 34071 601 SQUADRON is seen passing Raynes Park in the summer of 1963. *Keith Langston Collection*

Bulleid Light Pacific BR No 34071 601 SQUADRON is seen in 'Rebuilt' form whilst on shed at Nine Elms (70A) in the company of a sister locomotive and a pair of BR Standard Class 5 engines, late 1963. *Keith Langston Collection*

Bulleid Light Pacific BR No 34072 257 SQUADRON first ran in preservation for an amazing 12 years from 1990 to 2002.

The Southern Locomotives Limited owned Bulleid Light Pacific was stored out of use for a period and then put into the works in 2012 so that a comprehensive rebuild (major overhaul) can take place. When completed the locomotive will be returned to steam and then enter traffic for a third working life. The restoration of steam locomotives is a very complicated and costly business which is often dependent on public support. To check on progress of the work visit http://www.southern-locomotives.co.uk/34072/34072_appeal.html

Preserved Bulleid Light Pacific BR No 34072 257 SQUADRON is seen on a very grey June day at Swanage station, Dorset on that town's established heritage railway. *Keith Langston Collection*

34072 257 SQUADRON entered BR service April 1948 coupled to a 5500 gallon/5 ton capacity tender. Withdrawn by BR October 1964 and sent to Woodham Bros, Barry scrapyard but rescued for preservation in November 1984. **P**

257 Squadron was reformed as a fighter squadron on 17 May 1940 having been disbanded in June 1919. In early 1940 it was a Spitfire squadron but changed to Hurricanes, becoming operational in July 1940. The squadron remained in the south east of England during the whole of the 'Battle'.

Aircraft: Hawker Hurricane Mk.1.
Motto: Thay myay gyee shin shwe hti – 'Death or glory'.
Stations operated from, Hendon 17 May 1940, Northolt 4 July 1940, Debden 15 August 1940, Martlesham Heath 5 September 1940 and North Weald 8 October 1940.

The badge design incorporates a chinthe sejant. No 257 Squadron was the Burma gift squadron in World War II; the chinthe is a Burmese effigy.

British Railways (as a part of the British Transport Commission BTC) came into being on 1 January 1948. A programme of wholesale locomotive rebranding was put into place across all regions; accordingly, Bulleid Light Pacific BR No 34072 257 SQUADRON is seen in new BR Southern Region livery outside Brighton Works in the April of that year. Preserved locomotive is owned by Southern Locomotives Limited. *Rail Photoprints Collection*

BR Crests
Initially the name British Railways in full was added to locomotive liveries. During 1950 BR began gradually replacing the 'full name' style with a newly designed symbol now referred to as the BR 'early crest'. From 1956 onwards that design was replaced by a new design, now referred to as the BR 'late crest'. Each style attracted their own nickname, the early one being 'Lion on a Bike' and the later one being 'Ferret and Dartboard'.

BR Early Crest.

BR Late Crest.

Preserved Bulleid Light Pacific BR No 34072 257 SQUADRON is seen whilst positioning for its next departure, at Corfe Castle on the Swanage Railway in June 2001. *Keith Langston Collection*

Bulleid Light Pacific BR No 34072 257 SQUADRON is seen whilst about to leave Woking with the 09.30 Waterloo–Bournemouth West, on 3 March 1963. Note the amount of 'slack' in the tender full of coal, the fireman would have had to work hard keeping a good head of steam with that! *Ian Turnbull/Rail Photoprints Collection*

34073 249 SQUADRON entered BR service May 1948 coupled to a 5500 gallon/5 ton capacity tender. Withdrawn by BR June 1964 and sent to Woodham Bros, Barry scrapyard but rescued for preservation in February 1988. **P N**

249 Squadron was reformed as a fighter squadron on 16 May 1940, having been disbanded in October 1919. In early 1940 it was a Spitfire squadron but changed to Hurricanes, becoming operational in July 1940. After flying defensive patrols, it moved south in August and remained there throughout the 'Battle'.

Aircraft: Hawker Hurricane Mk.1.
Motto: Pugnis et Calcibus – 'With Fists and Heels'.
Stations operated from, Leconfield 18 May 1940, Church Fenton 8 July 1940, Boscombe Down 14 August 1940 and North Weald 1 September 1940.

The badge design incorporates an elephant passant. The elephant is in recognition of the squadron's association with the Gold Coast, as No 249 Squadron was one of the wartime gift squadrons.

Preserved Bulleid Light Pacific BR No 34073 249 SQUADRON is seen at Eastleigh depot (71A) in May 1964. The configuration of the front end air smoothed casing can clearly be appreciated in this study. Eastleigh locomotive depot was adjacent to the former railway workshops of the same name. The shed opened in 1903 and was one of the largest on the Southern Railway; it officially closed in 1967 but continued to be used for the storing and eventual scrapping of withdrawn locomotives. In 2007 the site was acquired by the private company Knights, Rail Services (KRS). *Jim Carter/Rail Photoprints Collection*

On 3 September 1936, B Flight of No 17 Squadron became No 46 Squadron at Kenley. The squadron was dispatched by aircraft carrier during April and May 1940 in order to fight out of an airfield in Norway. However, the move did not go according to plan and only after a second attempt were 10 Hurricane fighters eventually landed, but even then two of those aircraft crash landed onto adjacent marshy ground. Ordered back to the UK as the 'Battle' approached the aircraft successfully landed on the carrier HMS *Glorious*, off Norway, despite not being fitted with arrestor hooks!

Sadly, the carrier and her escorting destroyers HMS *Acasta* and HMS *Ardent* were sunk en route to Britain on June 8 1940 by the German battle cruisers *Scharnhorst* and *Gneisenau*, with the loss of over 1,500 lives.

However, the 46 Squadron ground crews returned to England safely aboard other ships and remarkably 46 Squadron was operational again by the end of June 1940.

Aircraft: Hurricane Mk.1.
Motto: 'We rise to conquer'.
Stations operated from, Digby 13 June 1940, Duxford 18 August 1940, Digby 19 August 1940 and Stapleford Tawney 1 September 1940. The arrows in the badge design signify speed in getting into action and their position and number represent three aircraft climbing.

Bulleid Light Pacific BR No 34074 46 SQUADRON is seen leaving London Victoria station with a boat train for Dover circa 1955, note the electrified '3rd rails'. Victoria is the nearest mainline station to Buckingham Palace and it was a major departure point for international travel, with boat trains regularly leaving there for Dover and Folkestone. Those services were discontinued in 1994 when the Eurostar began operating. *Dave Cobbe Collection/Rail Photoprints Collection*

Bulleid Light Pacific BR No 34074 46 SQUADRON in malachite livery is seen in charge of a down light loaded train at Shortlands on an unspecified date between entering BR service in May 1948 and being named 46 SQUADRON in May 1950. *Mike Morant Collection*

Bullied Light Pacific BR No 34074 46 SQUADRON passes Shorncliffe with an up service for London Victoria, on 7 August 1956. *Rail Photoprints Collection*

264 Squadron reformed on 30 October 1939 having been disbanded in March 1919. The squadron fought during the German invasion of the Low Countries. Flying Defiant two seat fighters the squadron suffered heavy losses in daytime combat and was consequently switched to night fighting in August 1940.

Aircraft: Boulton Paul Defiant Mk 1.
Motto: 'We defy'.

Stations operated from, Duxford 10 May 1940, Fowlmere 3 July 1940, Kirton-in-Lindsey 23 July 1940, Hornchurch 22 August 1940, Rochford 27 August 1940, Kirton-in-Lindsey 28 August 1940 and Rochford 29 October 1940.

The armorial helmet incorporated in the badge design indicates a readiness to fight.

Bulleid Light Pacific BR No 34075 264 SQUADRON is seen on shed at Exmouth Junction in 1964; note that by this time the nameplates and crests have been removed. The Exmouth Junction shed code was 72A, and then became 83C in September 1963. *Keith Langston Collection*

Below: Bulleid Light Pacific BR No 34075 264 SQUADRON is seen with other locomotives at the end of their working lives, whilst awaiting the cutting torch at Birds, Bridgend in June 1966. *Rail Photoprints Collection*

34076 41 SQUADRON entered BR service June 1948 coupled to a 5500 gallon/5 ton capacity tender. Withdrawn by BR January 1966 and cut up by John Cashmore, Newport November 1966.

41 Squadron flew defensive patrols at the onset of the war and in May 1940 moved south to fly covering operations over the Dunkirk beaches. The squadron alternated between Yorkshire and the south east during the 'Battle'.

Aircraft: Supermarine Spitfire Mk 1.
Motto: 'Seek and destroy'.
Stations operated from, Catterick 8 June 1940, Hornchurch 26 July 1940, Catterick 8 August 1940 and Hornchurch 3 September 1940.

Badge design, a double-armed cross; approved by HM King George VI in February 1937. The badge originated from the Squadron's association with St. Omer, France during World War I, the cross being part of the town's arms.

Bulleid Light Pacific BR No 34076 41 SQUADRON is seen passing Tisbury Gates with a Plymouth–Salisbury semi-fast service, on 2 August 1958. *Hugh Ballantyne/Rail Photoprints*

Bulleid Light Pacific No 34076 41 SQUADRON is seen coming out of shed at Bournemouth (71B) in 1962. *Keith Langston Collection*

Bulleid Light Pacific BR No 34076 41 SQUADRON is seen in pristine condition at Eastleigh (then 71A) presumably following a works visit. The locomotive carries an Exmouth Junction (72A) shedplate where No 34076 was allocated from May 1957 to September 1964. Note the large pile of coal. *Mike Morant Collection*

Bulleid Light Pacific BR No 34076 41 SQUADRON is seen at Eastleigh (then 70D) in late 1965, note that the grimy looking locomotive is minus a shedplate. *Rail Photoprints Collection*

603 Squadron was operational in time to intercept the first German air raid on southern England and is credited with destroying the first enemy aircraft over Britain in WWII, it was also known as the City of Edinburgh Squadron. The squadron carried out defensive duties in Scotland before moving south in August 1940.

Aircraft: Supermarine Spitfire Mk 1.
Motto: Gin ye daur – 'If you dare'.
Stations operated from, Turnhouse 5 May 1940 and Hornchurch 27 August 1940.

The castle in the badge is similar to that in the Arms of the City of Edinburgh.

Rebuilt Bulleid Light Pacific BR No 34077 603 SQUADRON is seen on the turntable at Nine Elms depot (70A), circa 1965. Great apartments for railway enthusiasts but perhaps not so good for keeping drying washing free of soot, especially when the prevailing wind was from the direction of the steam depot! *Keith Langston Collection*

Rebuilt Bulleid Light Pacific BR No 34077 603 SQUADRON is seen at Bournemouth (then 70F) in the summer of 1965. Note that the locomotive is shorn of nameplate and crest and also carries a hand painted smoke box number plate. *Rail Photoprints Collection*

Bulleid Light Pacific BR No 34077 603 SQUADRON speeds through Paddock Wood station in this undated view. *Mike Morant Collection*

Bulleid Light Pacific BR No 34077 603 SQUADRON is seen in malachite livery outside Brighton Works in August 1948. *Rail Photoprints Collection*

Bulleid Light Pacific BR No 34077 603 SQUADRON is seen passing Tonbridge at speed on 26 May 1958. *Ian Turnbull/Rail Photoprints Collection*

The view from the cab. Rebuilt Bulleid Light Pacific BR No 34077 603 SQUADRON prepares to leave London Waterloo in this 1964 image. *Keith Langston Collection*

34078 222 SQUADRON entered BR service July 1948 coupled to a 5500 gallon/5 ton capacity tender. Withdrawn by BR September 1964 and cut up by Birds, Morriston December 1964. **N**

222 Squadron was reformed in October 1939 having been disbanded in May 1919. At first flying Blenheims it was equipped with Spitfires in March 1940. The squadron provided cover during the Dunkirk evacuations and defended the south east of England during the last part of the 'Battle'.

Aircraft: Supermarine Spitfire Mk 1.
*Motto: Pambili bo (*from the *Zulu) –* 'Go straight ahead'.
Stations operated from, Kirton in Lindsay 4 June 1939 and Hornchurch 29 August 1940.

The Wildebeest incorporated in the badge design comes from the armorial bearings of Natal, the squadron being the Natal gift squadron; the Wildebeest also symbolises speed.

Bulleid Light Pacific BR No 34078 222 SQUADRON is seen at Wadebridge with the down 'Atlantic Coast Express' (11.00 from London Waterloo). The date was 1 July 1964, on that occasion a train headboard was not carried. *Dave Cobbe/Rail Photoprints Collection. Inset:* A nameplate from Bulleid Light Pacific BR No 34078 222 SQUADRON, seen as displayed at Manston Museum, in Kent UK.

141 Squadron was initially formed in January 1918, disbanded in February 1920 and reformed in October 1939. '141' was dealt a big blow when in early 1940 six aircraft out of a nine aircraft patrol were shot down over the channel, in a daytime encounter with Me 109 fighters. The squadron was withdrawn to Scotland as their Defiant fighters were judged to be no match for the German single seat attack planes, during daytime. The squadron returned south in September/October 1940 in order to operate night patrols.

Aircraft: Boulton Paul Defiant Mk1.
Motto: Caedimus noctu – 'We stay by night'.
Stations operated from, Turnhouse 28 June 1940, West Malling 12 July 1940, Prestwick 21 July 1940, Dyce and Montrose 22 August 1940, Turnhouse 30 August 1940, Biggin Hill 13 September to 18 September 1940, Gatwick 18 September to 22 October 1940, Drem 15 October 1940 and Gatwick 24 October 1940.

The badge design incorporates a leopard's face on an ogress – symbolizing fighting in the dark.

The very smartly turned out Bullied Light Pacific BR No 34079 141 SQUADRON arrives at Bristol Temple Meads with the stock for a Warwickshire Railway Society special from Bristol to Derby and Crewe, on 14 June 1964. The tour itinerary allowed passengers the opportunity to visit Derby Works, Crewe Works and Crewe North shed (5A). *Hugh Ballantyne/Rail Photoprints*

Bulleid Light Pacific BR No 34079 141 SQUADRON passes through Swanwick with the diverted 10.00 Weymouth–Waterloo service on 8 November 1964. *Ian Turnbull/Rail Photoprints Collection*

Bulleid Light Pacific BR No 34080 74 SQUADRON is seen passing Worting Junction signalbox whilst in charge of the 10.08 Bournemouth to London Waterloo express service. The date was 8 August 1964, only a month before the locomotives recorded withdrawn date. *Mike Morant Collection*

34080 74 SQUADRON entered BR service August 1948 coupled to a 5500 gallon/5 ton capacity tender. Withdrawn by BR September 1964 cut up by Birds, Morriston December 1964.

74 Squadron flew defensive patrols during the opening phase of the war and later covered the evacuation at Dunkirk. The squadron was active during the first period of the 'Battle' and was then withdrawn in August 1940 for 'rest', returning south in mid October.

Aircraft: Supermarine Spitfire Mk 1 (later Spitfire Mk.11a).
Motto: I fear no man.
Stations operated from, Hornchurch 25 June 1940, Wittering 14 August 1940, Kirton-in-Lindsey 21 August 1940, Coltishall 9 September 1940 and Biggin Hill 15 October 1940.

The badge design which was approved for use by HM King George VI in February 1937 incorporated a tiger's face.

Bulleid Light Pacific BR No 34080 74 SQUADRON is seen passing Raynes Park with a down Bournemouth service on 23 August 1962. *Rail Photoprints Collection*

Bulleid Light Pacific BR No 34080 74 SQUADRON is seen approaching the west portal of Honiton Tunnel as it heads an eastbound freight, in July 1956. Note the coal which has completely missed the tender hopper and is sitting on the train air brake reservoirs. *David Anderson.*

34081 92 SQUADRON entered BR service September 1948 coupled to a 5500 gallon/5 ton capacity tender. Withdrawn by BR August 1984 and sent to be cut up by Woodham Bros, Barry but rescued for preservation during autumn 1973. **P**

92 Squadron reformed 10 October 1939 at Tangmere, having been disbanded on 7 August 1919. First equipped with Blenheims the squadron converted to Spitfires in March 1940 (operational 9 May). After flying patrols over France in May/June the squadron carried out defensive duties over South Wales, in September it joined '11 Group' for the final phase of the 'Battle'.

Aircraft: Supermarine Spitfire Mk 1.
Motto: Aut pugna aut morere – 'Either fight or die'. Stations operated from, Pembrey 18 June 1940 and Biggin Hill 8 September 1940.

The badge design incorporates a Cobra entwining a sprig of maple leaf. The maple leaf signifies the squadron's association as a Canadian unit in the First World War. The Cobra represents the fact that No 92 was one of the East India gift squadrons in World War II.

Preserved Bulleid Light Pacific BR No 34081 92 SQUADRON is seen during an April 2007 visit to the Llangollen Railway. The locomotive is owned by the 'Battle of Britain Locomotive Society'.
Fred Kerr

Nameplate and crest of Preserved Bulleid Light Pacific BR No 34081 92 SQUADRON. *Keith Langston Collection*

Preserved Bulleid Light Pacific BR No 34081 92 SQUADRON with an infrastructure (permanent way) train is pictured on a beautiful summer's day at the Bluebell Railway in 1992. *Paul Pettitt*

34082 615 SQUADRON entered BR service September 1948 coupled to a 5500 gallon/5 ton capacity tender. **R** April 1960. Withdrawn by BR April 1966 and cut up by John Cashmore, Newport September 1966. **N**

615 Squadron flew Gladiator aircraft over France as a contingent of the British Expeditionary Forces, it was also known as the County of Surrey Squadron. The squadron began converting to Hurricanes in April 1940 and after returning to Britain took part in the opening stages of the 'Battle' before moving to Scotland at the end of August to rest and re-equip, returning south in October 1940.

Aircraft: Hawker Hurricane Mk 1.
Motto: Conjunctis viribus – 'By our united force'.
Stations operated from, Kenley 20 May 1940, Prestwick 29 August 1940 and Northolt 10 October 1940.

The badge incorporates an oak sprig, on a star of six points.

Bulleid Light Pacific BR No 34082 615 SQUADRON is seen at Bournemouth shed (71B), on 27 May 1965. *Rail Photoprints Collection*

BR era shedplates came into being with the nationalisation of the railways (1948). Locomotives of all regions normally had a cast iron plate fixed onto their smokebox door with a letter and number(s) to readily identify their home shed. In modern times shedplates have become highly collectable items.

Shedplate for 71B Bournemouth, in use between 1948 and September 1963.

34083 605 SQUADRON entered BR service October 1948 coupled to a 5500 gallon/5 ton capacity tender. Withdrawn by BR June 1964 cut up by Birds, Bridgend between June 1965 and June 1966.

605 Squadron, having originally recruited in the West Midlands was known as the County of Warwick Squadron and originally flew as a bomber unit. Re-designated a fighter squadron, and operating from Tangmere in 1939, the squadron flew a mix of Gladiators and Hurricanes. When re-equipped with Hurricanes the squadron moved to Scotland in February 1940, and then moved back south in September 1940 for the closing stages of the 'Battle'.

Aircraft: Hawker Hurricane Mk 1.
Motto: Nunquam dormio – 'I never sleep'.
Stations operated from, Drem 28 May 1940 and Croydon 7 September 1940.

The badge incorporates a bear supporting a ragged staff. The device on the badge has long been associated with Warwickshire.

Bulleid Light Pacific BR No 34083 605 SQUADRON is seen passing Abbotscliffe whilst heading away from Folkestone with an up boat train on 6 August 1956. To accommodate the often large amount of passenger luggage boat trains would often have an appropriate van included in the consist, and one such vehicle can be identified immediately behind the locomotive. *Rail Photoprints Collection*

253 Squadron reformed at Manston on 30 October 1939 having been disbanded 31 May 1919. The squadron was to become a shipping protection unit equipped with Blenheims but in reality never received any, instead Hurricanes were allocated and it became operational on 3 April 1940. The squadron operated over France in May 1940 and later after re-equipping took part in the 'Battle' from August onwards.

Aircraft: Hawker Hurricane Mk 1.
Motto: 'Come one, come all'.
Stations operated from, Kirton-in-Lindsey 24 May 1940, Turnhouse 21 July 1940, Prestwick 23 August 1940, Kenley 29 August 1940 and Kenley 16 September 1940.

The back of a dexter bowed arm clad in Mogul armour, the hand holding an Indian battle-axe. The squadron became the Hyderabad gift squadron accordingly the badge was suggested by the Nizam of Hyderabad as being appropriate.

The two contrasting Bulleid Light Pacific styles are shown to good effect in this image taken at Exeter Central in August 1964. Seen in original condition is 'Battle of Britain' class BR No 34084 253 SQUADRON is stood at the platform with a single coach (brake) whilst rebuilt 'West Country' class BR No 34039 BOSCASTLE is seen on the adjacent road taking water. *Hugh Ballantyne/Rail Photoprints*

Bulleid Light Pacific BR No 34084 253 SQUADRON is seen at Eastleigh, on 27 February 1965. *Rail Photoprints Collection*

On February 20 1960 Bulleid Light Pacific BR No 34084 253 SQUADRON suffered a serious derailment when it failed to stop at the end of the up goods loop and took a tumble down the embankment. This undated image was taken within a few days of the incident *Mike Morant Collection*

Note that the locomotive's side sheeting had been removed and packing in the form of wooden sleepers had been put in place prior to up righting the engine. Although looking badly damaged the engineers decreed that No 34084 was only superficially damaged, and thus returned to traffic following overhaul at Eastleigh works in April 1960. The locomotive went on to serve BR/SR almost to the end of the steam era.

'Atlantic Coast Express'. London Waterloo-Padstow/Ilfracombe/Bude and others first ran on 19 July 1926. Title suspended 10 September 1939 and reinstated 6 October 1947, and this trains last titled run took place on 5 September 1964.

34085 501 SQUADRON entered BR service November 1948 coupled to a 5500 gallon/5 ton capacity tender. **R** June 1960. Withdrawn by BR September 1965 and cut up by J. Buttigieg, Newport April 1966. **N**

Originally 501 Squadron flew defensive patrols from the outbreak of war until May 1940 when it transferred to France to provide fighter cover for the AASF*, it was also known as the County of Gloucester Squadron. After the surrender of France, the squadron returned to Britain and was based in southern England for the whole of the 'Battle'.

Aircraft: Hawker Hurricane Mk 1.
Motto: 'Nil time'.
Stations operated from, Croydon 21 June 1940, Middle Wallop 4 July 1940, Gravesend 25 July 1940 and Kenley 10 1940.

The badge design incorporated a boar's head taken from the Gloucester coat of arms. The wild boar is an animal also noted for its courage.

*The AASF consisted of RAF light bomber squadrons based within France (around Rheims) to allow them to bomb Germany should the political decision to do so be taken. When the German offensive in the West began on 10 May 1940, and thereafter the AASF bomber force was used against the advancing German Army and its lines of communications. The AASF was part of the BAFF (British Air Force in France).

Rebuilt Bulleid Light Pacific BR No 34085 501 SQUADRON is seen leaving Oxford with a southbound 'Pines Express' service, during May 1965. *David Anderson*

The Pines Express/Pines Express
Introduced 7 May 1928 – Title withdrawn 9 September 1939 and reinstated 23 May 1949. Last titled run 4 March 1967.
Manchester London Road–Bournemouth West via Bath and the S&D route until 8 September 1962. Manchester Piccadilly–Bournemouth West via Oxford and Southampton until 3 October 1965.
Manchester Piccadilly–Poole from 4 October 1965.
Manchester London Road renamed Manchester Piccadilly 12 September 1960.

Bulleid Light Pacific BR No 34085 501 SQUADRON is seen in charge of the down Golden Arrow at Purley Oaks, on the Brighton mainline whilst using a temporary diversionary route during 1960. *Mike Morant Collection*

Rebuilt Bulleid Light Pacific BR No 34085 501 SQUADRON is seen at Nine Elms (70A) circa 1962. At that time the locomotive was carrying a Bournemouth (71B) shedplate. *Rail Photoprints Collection*

34086 219 SQUADRON entered BR service December 1948 coupled to a 5500 gallon/5 ton capacity tender. Withdrawn by BR June 1966 and cut up by J. Buttigieg, Newport November 1966. **N**

219 Squadron was reformed at Catterick 4 October 1939 having been disbanded 7 February 1919. Becoming operational on 21 February 1940 it was fully employed on night defence duties. In October 1940 the squadron moved south to protect London and towards end of 'Battle' began the conversion to Beaufighters.

Aircraft: Bristol Blenheim Mk 1F and Bristol Beaufighter Mk 1F.
Motto: 'From dusk till dawn'.
Stations operated from Catterick 4 October 1939 and Redhill 12 October 1940

The badge design incorporates a Death's Head Hawk Moth.

Bulleid Light Pacific BR No 34086 219 SQUADRON prepares to leave Oxford with the 08.30 Newcastle-Bournemouth West service on 17 July 1956. *Ian Turnbull/ Rail Photoprints Collection*

Bulleid Light Pacific BR No 34086 219 SQUADRON is seen in a very grimy condition at Exmouth Junction (72A) in 1963. *Keith Langston Collection*

In complete contrast Bulleid Light Pacific BR No 34086 219 SQUADRON is seen in near pristine condition whilst being readied for Golden Arrow service at Dover in July 1960. *Rail Photoprints Collection*

34087 145 SQUADRON entered BR service December 1948 coupled to a 5500 gallon/5 ton capacity tender. **R** December 1960. Withdrawn by BR July 1967 and cut up by John Cashmore, Newport between April and September 1968.

145 Squadron was reformed at Croydon on 10 October 1939 as a fighter squadron, having been disbanded 2 September 1919. Re-equipped with Hurricanes it became operational in May 1940 and flew patrols over Northern France. After covering the Dunkirk evacuations, the squadron took part in the early stages of the 'Battle' moving to Scotland in mid-August but returning south in October 1940.

Aircraft: Hawker Hurricane Mk 1.
Motto: Diu noctuque pugnamus – 'We fight by day and night'.
Stations operated from, Tangmere 10 May 1940, Westhampnett 31 July 1940, Drem 14 August 1940, Dyce 3 August 1940 and Tangmere 9 October 1940.

The badge design incorporates a sword in bend, point downward in front of a cross. The sword represents No 145 Squadron's role, and the cross the squadron's association with No 14 Squadron.

Nocturne at Eastleigh on 25 May 1965. Rebuilt Bulleid Light Pacific BR No 34087 145 SQUADRON is seen with WC Light Pacific No 34013 OKEHAMPTON. By that time the 'Battle of Britain' class engine had not only lost its nameplate and crest but also the mounting bracket. *Jim Carter/Rail Photoprints Collection*

Bulleid Light Pacific BR No 34087 145 SQUADRON is seen leaning to the curve at Gillingham on 25 April 1954. *Mike Morant Collection*

Rebuilt Bulleid Light Pacific BR No 34087 145 SQUADRON is seen with a sister locomotive at Bournemouth depot (then 70F) at 3.00AM on 4 April 1967. Note that the nameplates, crests and fixing frames have been removed from these shed mates. *Brian Robbins/Rail Photoprints Collection*

34088 213 SQUADRON entered BR service December 1948 coupled to a 5500 gallon/5 ton capacity tender. **R** April 1960. Withdrawn by BR March 1967 and cut up by John Cashmore, Newport March 1968.

213 Squadron was reformed at Northolt on 8 March 1937 having been disbanded in December 1919, the squadron later moved to Yorkshire. It flew sorties over France in support of the British Expeditionary Force (BEF) and then moved south in early June 1940, remaining in the south west and southern England, for the duration of the 'Battle'.

Aircraft: Hawker Hurricane Mk 1.
Motto: Irritatus lacessit crabro – 'The hornet attacks when roused'.
Stations operated from, Exeter 18 June 1940 and Tangmere 7 September 1940.

The badge design incorporates a Hornet.

Bulleid Light Pacific BR No 34088 213 SQUADRON receives the final touches as a headboard is fitted in preparation for the working of a special train in connection with visiting heads of state, note the burnished buffers. 'WC' class Locomotive No 34017 ILFRACOMBE has been prepared as the standby motive power, location Stewarts Lane (73A), circa 1956. *Rail Photoprints Collection*

Rebuilt Bulleid Light Pacific BR No 34088 213 SQUADRON approaches Worting flyover as it heads a Waterloo–Bournemouth service, on 24 September 1966. *Richard Lewis/ Rail Photoprints*

Rebuilt Bulleid Light Pacific BR No 34088 213 SQUADRON carefully negotiates the curve through Smitham station with the 1963 royal Derby Day races special train (note the Royal Train 4 disc head code). The stock consisted of a royal saloon and three Pullman cars. *Mike Morant Collection*

Rebuilt Bulleid Light Pacific BR No 34088 213 SQUADRON in ex works condition ambles, tender first, through Kingswood & Burgh Heath station, whilst hauling the 29 May 1963 Derby Day royal train stock empty coaching stock (ECS). Note that the headcode has been changed. *Mike Morant Collection*

34089 602 SQUADRON entered BR service December 1948 coupled to a 5500 gallon/5 ton capacity tender. **R** November 1960. Withdrawn by BR July 1967 and cut up by John Cashmore, Newport between April and September 1968. **N**

602 Squadron was equipped with Spitfires in May 1939 and was utilised intercepting Luftwaffe bombing raids over Scotland, also known as the City of Glasgow Squadron. At the start of the 'Battle' 602 was still based north of the border but moved south in mid August 1940.

Aircraft: Supermarine Spitfire Mk 1.
Motto: Cave leonem cruciatum 'Beware the tormented lion'.
Stations operated from, Drem 28 May 1940 and Westhampnett 13 August 1940.

The badge design incorporates a lion rampant in front of a white saltire. The lion was adopted in view of the squadron's association with Scotland and likewise the saltire to represent the cross of St Andrew.

Rebuilt Bulleid Light Pacific BR No 34089 602 SQUADRON is seen between Beaulieu Road and Lyndhurst Road, in the New Forest with the 13.30 Waterloo–Weymouth, on 28 March 1967. Note that the locomotive had already lost its nameplate and crest but still retained the mounting frame. *Dave Rostance/Rail Photoprints Collection*

Bulleid Light Pacific BR No 34089 602 SQUADRON is seen near Shorncliffe with the up Golden Arrow, circa 1950. *Rail Photoprints Collection*

Rebuilt Bulleid Light Pacific BR No 34089 602 SQUADRON is seen at Eastleigh (70D) in April 1965. *Rail Photoprints Collection*

34090 SIR EUSTACE MISSENDEN, Southern Railway entered BR service January 1949 coupled to a 5500 gallon/5 ton capacity tender. **R** August 1960. Withdrawn by BR July 1967 cut up by John Cashmore, Newport March 1968.

Although no direct military link existed between Sir Eustace Missenden and the RAF this locomotive was nevertheless included in those chosen to be part of the 'Battle of Britain' class. It was so named because Sir Eustace was the war time General Manager of the Southern Railway. Additionally, the words Southern Railway were added to the name (although in letters of a smaller size) to commemorate the fact that the men and women of the Southern played a significant part in 'The Finest Hour', and in particular to honour those who lost their lives.

On 15 September 1940 a damaged Hurricane aircraft of 229 Squadron crashed onto the Staplehurst railway station. As a result, the Belgian pilot Georges Doutrepont died as did 18-year-old Southern Railway booking clerk Charles Ashdown. A memorial was unveiled at the station in 2003 and the ceremony was performed by Eric Doutrepont, son of Georges, accordingly the Belgian Air Force performed a flypast. As unveiled the plaque mistakenly recorded the railway company as being 'Southern Railway**s**', the plural s having been being incorrectly added.

Bulleid Light Pacific BR No 34090 SIR EUSTACE MISSENDEN, SOUTHERN RAILWAY, is seen near Sandling with an up Boat Train (the train includes two luggage vans and the passenger coaches are 'Pullman' stock) for London Victoria, circa 1953. Note the unique style of nameplate and crest, this was the only 'Battle of Britain' class locomotive to carry a name and crest in that style. Rail Photoprints Collection

Bulleid Light Pacific BR No 34090 SIR EUSTACE MISSENDEN SOUTHERN RAILWAY makes a fine sight whilst climbing away from Folkestone Boat Train Sidings, in June 1951. Both members of the footplate crew seemed keen to be in the picture! *Rail Photoprints Collection*

Bulleid Light Pacific BR No 34090 SIR EUSTACE MISSENDEN, SOUTHERN RAILWAY, is seen in BR malachite livery on the outskirts of Sandling, circa 1953. *Rail Photoprints Collection*

Rebuilt Bulleid Light Pacific BR No 34090 SIR EUSTACE MISSENDEN, SOUTHERN RAILWAY, (minus nameplates) waits at Eastleigh station in 1967. Note the wooden 'boats' of fresh produce, being loaded/unloaded, which carry the words 'More top grade Dutch Tomatoes for FW Woolworth & Co', now there is a real British blast from the past! The train member of station staff is sporting a white floral token in his buttonhole, whilst the young porter has a very 60s hair style in this atmospheric image. *Keith Langston Collection*

Bulleid Light Pacific BR No 34090 SIR EUSTACE MISSENDEN, SOUTHERN RAILWAY is seen at Shorncliffe. This was a BR Brighton built locomotive and it survived right until the end of SR steam. *Mike Morant Collection*

Rebuilt Bulleid Light Pacific BR No 34090 SIR EUSTACE MISSENDEN, SOUTHERN RAILWAY, takes water at Southampton Central station whilst heading a Weymouth–Waterloo service in 1962. *Jim Carter/Rail Photoprints Collection*

34109 SIR TRAFFORD LEIGH-MALLORY entered BR service May 1950 coupled to a 5500 gallon/5 ton capacity tender. **R** March 1961. Withdrawn by BR September 1964 cut up by Birds, Morriston December 1966. **N**

Sir Trafford Leigh- Mallory KCB, DSO & Bar (11 July 1892–14 November 1944).

During the pre-Second World War build-up Sir Trafford Leigh-Mallory was Air Officer Commanding (AOC) No. 12 (Fighter) Group. Shortly after the end of the Battle of Britain, Mallory took over command of No. 11 (Fighter) Group. In 1942 he became the Commander-in-Chief (C-in-C) of Fighter Command before being selected in 1943 to be the C-in-C of the Allied Expeditionary Air Force, and thus the air commander for the Allied Invasion of Normandy.

In November 1944, whilst en route to Ceylon to take up the post of Air Commander-in-Chief South East Asia Command (SEAC), the 'Avro York' aircraft he was travelling in crashed in the French Alps. Leigh-Mallory, his wife and eight others were killed. He was one of the most senior British officers and the most senior RAF officer to be killed in the Second World War.

Rebuilt Bulleid Light Pacific BR No 34109 SIR TRAFFORD LEIGH – MALLORY backs onto Weymouth shed (then 71G) for servicing, in July 1963. *Rail Photoprints Collection*

34110 66 SQUADRON entered BR service January 1951 coupled to a 5500 gallon/5 ton capacity tender. Withdrawn by BR November 1963 cut up at BR Eastleigh Works March 1964.

66 Squadron was reformed at Duxford from C Flight of 19 Squadron, on 20 July 1936 with Gloster Gauntlet aircraft. The squadron was re-equipped with Spitfires in November 1938 and after the outbreak of war it flew defensive duties until 1940 when it was transferred in order to fly covering patrols over Dunkirk. The squadron remained in the south east for the duration of the 'Battle'.

Aircraft: Supermarine Spitfire Mk 1.
Motto: Cavete praemonui – 'Beware, I have warned'.
Stations operated from, Coltishall 29 May 1940, Kenley 3 September 1940, Gravesend 11 September 1940, and West Malling 30 October 1940.

The badge design incorporates a rattlesnake, which typifies aggressive spirit and striking power.

General note: It is appreciated that many squadrons could have been re-equipped with other aircraft types over the duration of the war, but this listing details only those aircraft type recorded as being allocated during the period designated as 'The Battle of Britain'.

Bulleid Light Pacific BR No 34110 66 SQUADRON is seen at the locomotive's home shed Exmouth Junction (72A), in June 1962. Note the oil can on the buffer beam. Unlike the other 'BB' class locomotives No 34110 only carried a nameplate and no plaque, as can be clearly seen in this image. *Rail Photoprints Collection*

Bulleid Light Pacific BR No 34110 66 SQUADRON approaches journeys end at Padstow with a service from Waterloo while an unidentified 'N' Class is turned on the turntable, circa 1959. *Alan H. Bryant ARPS/Rail Photoprints Collection*

Preserved Bulleid Light Pacific 'Battle of Britain' class locomotives

Locomotive	Name	Home base/status August 2017
34051	WINSTON CHURCHILL	National Rail Museum – Static Display
34053	SIR KEITH PARK R	Swanage Railway – Operational
34058	SIR FREDERICK PILE R	Mid-Hants Railway – Under Restoration
34059	SIR ARCHIBALD SINCLAIR R	Bluebell Railway – Operational
34067	TANGMERE	Operational mainline certified
34070	MANSTON	Swanage Railway – Operational
34072	257 SQUADRON	Swanage Railway- Undergoing repair
34073	249 SQUADRON	West Coast Railways – Under Restoration
34081	92 SQUADRON	Nene Valley Railway – Under Restoration

The operational status and location of preserved locomotives are often subject to change. It may be prudent to check before arranging visits.

Class Details

'BB' Class SR Bulleid Light Pacific 6MT reclassified 7P5F in 1953*	4-6-2	16 built 1945–1951 At Brighton Works	Driving Wheel 6ft 2ins dia.	3 – cylinders Bulleid piston valves Rebuilt Walschaert piston valves	Working BP 280psi Superheated Tractive effort 31050lbf Later reduced to 250psi Superheated Tractive effort 27715lbf

* Rebuilt locomotives reclassified 7P6F in 1961.

The driver of Rebuilt Bulleid Light Pacific BR No 34081 92 SQUADRON waits for 'the road', a night time study taken at the Bluebell Railway on 19 October 2007.
Paul Pettitt

https://www.youtube.com/watch?v=ZqPdSpezHhg
The Battle of Britain (1943) 53min documentary.

Chapter 4

BRITISH RAILWAYS –
THE STANDARD DESIGN GROUP

In 1948 British Railways (BR) under the auspices of the British Transport Commission (BTC) was created. The new organisation set about the mammoth task of modernising the country's locomotive fleet following WWII. Within BR a new division called the Standard Design Group was created and given a mandate to solve the operational problems caused by steam motive power shortages across the regions. They were to do so by introducing a new series of easily maintained locomotives with common design features.

In the first instance the 'Group' set about evaluating the engines of the old 'Big Four' in order to decide which, if any, of their characteristics would be of use in the planned new designs. To help in the decision-making process locomotive exchanges between the regions of British Railways took place, during which a very comprehensive amount of operating and performance related data was collected. In the final analysis of all the locomotive designs which were trialled the Stanier designed locomotives (of the former LMS) were said to have impressed the group's team leader the most.

Varying numbers of the 12 individual BR Standard Class locomotives were built at Brighton, Crewe, Darlington, Derby, Doncaster, Horwich and Swindon locomotive works. In total 999 Standard Class engines were built between 1951 and 1958, of those 769 were tender types and 230 tank engines.

Robert Arthur Riddles CBE

The man chosen to lead the group was Robert Arthur Riddles (born in 1892) who trained as an apprentice with London North Western Railway (LNWR) at Crewe Works between 1909 and 1913. After war service his first two senior positions within the railway industry were firstly Assistant to the Works Manager Crewe, and then Progress Assistant to the Works Manager between 1920 and 1928. Riddles also served at Derby Works and later in Glasgow with LMS Scotland.

In 1940 he was appointed to the role of Director of Transportation Equipment, Ministry of Supply and in 1941 became Deputy Director General of that organisation. In 1943 he returned to the LMS as Chief Stores Superintendent, and was in that year awarded the CBE. Riddles was promoted first to Vice President Engineering in 1946 and then to Chief Mechanical and Electrical Engineer (CME) for British Railways in 1948. He retired from BR on 30 September 1953 and died in June 1983.

BR Standard 'Britannia Class' File 70046A

The first of the 'Riddles' Standard type locomotive classes to enter service was the 7P6F (7MT) 4-6-2 (Pacific) BR Standard 'Britannia' class. A total of 55 engines of the 2-cylinder design were built, all of them at Crewe Works. The first of the class being No 70000 BRITANNIA which entered service in January 1951. All but one of the locomotives were given names and amongst those were 9 with a direct (modern day) military connection, a further 9 given names with an historical military link. In all cases the cast nameplates were carried on the smoke deflectors.

From 1948 until the mid-1950s the responsibility for selecting BR steam locomotive names rested with a specially created Locomotive Naming Committee, which consisted of three senior railway officials. Whilst the committee made

The front end of BR Standard 'Britannia' class No 70046 ANZAC, seen at Stockport in April 1960. *Keith Langston Collection*

known a preference for names of heroes and historically important people, they stated that they were keen to resist names or associations with the military. Their first task was to choose names for 'Britannia' Class locomotives, and interestingly that list did however, include names with military connections!

The gentleman credited with putting forward the suggestion that the BR 7P6F Pacific class be called 'Britannia' was the accomplished railway photographer, and much loved railway enthusiast Bishop Eric Treacy (1907–1978).

70000 BRITANNIA built Crewe Works, entered service January 1951 with a BR1 4250 gallon/7 ton tender, withdrawn from BR service June 1966. This locomotive is preserved. **P** At that time the name **BRITANNIA** was already in use, and was carried by LMS 'Jubilee' class locomotive BR No 45700. That engine was re-named **AMETHYST** in September 1951 to accommodate the aforementioned committee's choice.

Britannia is the ancient term for Great Britain and also the female personification of the island. The name is Latin and was derived from the Greek form Prettanike or Brettaniai which originally referred to the collection of individually named islands, which included Great Britain (Albion). After their AD 43 conquest of Britain the Romans also named their newly established province Britannia. The Latin name Britannia long survived the 5th century Roman withdrawal from Britain, and the eventual fall of the Roman Empire, becoming Britain in English and Prydain in modern Welsh. Britannia came to be personified as a warrior goddess, and was thereafter depicted armed with a trident, shield and wearing a centurion's helmet.

https://www.youtube.com/watch?v=4DXarVw6NgA
Preserved No 70000 BRITANNIA on Camberley Bank, 7 June 2012.

Preserved BR Standard 'Britannia' class 7P6F (alternatively 7MT-Mixed Traffic) Pacific No 70000 BRITANNIA, in January 2012 looking absolutely pristine at the end of an overhaul and repaint in BR Green livery by LNWR Heritage Ltd., Crewe, the white painting of the cab roof white is in keeping with a railway tradition for locomotives to be used on royal train duty. On 24 January 2012, BR Standard Pacific No 70000 hauled the royal train which conveyed HRH Prince of Wales from Preston to Wakefield. On arrival at Wakefield station HRH Prince Charles, Prince of Wales performed a renaming ceremony to commemorate the engine's recent return to traffic. After the   locomotive naming ceremony, the royal party visited the offices of publishers Pen & Sword Books, Barnsley. *Keith Langston Collection*

BR Standard No 70000 BRITANNIA is seen in the then recently applied BR Black livery (but minus nameplates) at LNWR Heritage Crewe during March 2011. To facilitate the haulage of modern mainline coaching stock, the locomotive has been fitted with air brake equipment, the pump for which can be seen inside the (left hand as pictured) smoke deflector. The associated air tanks are located under the tender. *Keith Langston Collection*

Preserved BR Standard No 70000 BRITANNIA is seen passing Gaerwen signal box on the Bangor–Holyhead section of the North Wales Coast route. This recreated 'Irish Mail' special train ran in July 1992. *Dave Jones*

70001 LORD HURCOMB built Crewe Works, entered service January 1951 with a BR1 4250 gallon/7 ton tender, withdrawn from BR service August 1966. Cut for scrap by Motherwell Machinery & Scrap, Wishaw in December 1966/ January 1967.

Cyril William Hurcomb, 1st Baron Hurcomb GCB, KBE (1883–1975) was a British civil servant. Lord Hurcomb was head of the Ministry of War Transport between 1941 and 1947, a period which included World War II and he was later the first chairman of the British Transport Commission (BTC) which he served between 1948 and 1953. His Lordship was a very keen ornithologist; accordingly, he played a key role in formulating and putting into law the 1954 Protection of Birds Act. He served for a period as chairman of the Royal Society for the Protection of Birds and went on to become president of that society. He was elevated to the peerage as Baron Hurcomb in July 1950.

When newly introduced the 'Standard Britannia Pacific' class locomotives worked express passenger services over most of the principal main lines. They made a big impact with both the railway fraternity, travelling public and enthusiasts. Indeed, this author well recalls boyhood Britannia spotting weekend trips to Crewe station for a sight of ex works locomotives on the North shed (5A) during the Spring and summer of 1951. Their distinctive high running plates, two outside cylinders, with Walschaert valve gear made them easily recognisable. They were generally well received but the BR Western Region engine crews were initially less keen to embrace the type because of their left-hand drive configuration which was at variance with historic GWR practice.* When first introduced there were initial problems in traffic which were overcome by modifications. Notably, the class worked extremely well over the difficult ex Great Eastern Railway (GER) routes where they appreciably improved timekeeping, through reliability, and allowed improvements to the timetable. As the planned demise of steam traction got underway the Britannia Pacifics were gradually ousted from the other BR regions and mainly finished their working lives on the London Midland Region where they were often relegated to freight duties.

 *See *British Steam-BR Standard Locomotives* published by Pen & Sword Books Ltd., 2012

BR Standard 'Britannia' class 7MT Pacific No 70001 LORD HURCOMB has steam in hand, and makes an impressive sight departing Wickham Market station. The aforementioned station is located on the Ipswich–Lowestoft, East Suffolk mainline, and is actually some 2 miles from Wickham Market. *Dr. Ian C. Allen/ Transport Treasury*

70007 COEUR-DE-LION built Crewe Works, entered service April 1951 with a BR1 4250 gallon/7 ton tender, withdrawn from BR service June 1965. Cut for scrap at Crewe Works (BR) in July 1965.

Cœur de Lion, or Richard the Lionheart, (1157–1199). Richard I earned his well-used epithet even before his accession to the throne, no doubt because of his reputation as a great military leader and warrior. He was King of England from 6 July 1189 until his death. He also ruled as Duke of Normandy, Duke of Aquitaine, Duke of Gascony, Lord of Cyprus, Count of Anjou, Count of Maine, Count of Nantes, and Overlord of Brittany at various times during the same period. He actually spent little time in England and in fact spoke only French; between battles he mainly resided at his ancestral home in the Duchy of Aquitaine in the southwest of France.

BR Standard 'Britannia' class 7MT Pacific No 70007 COEUR-DE-LION is pictured prior to departure from London Liverpool Street station with a train for East Anglia in 1958. Both images Michael Bentley Collection

BR Standard 'Britannia' class 7MT Pacific No 70007 COEUR-DE-LION is seen at Crewe North (5A) on 18 March 1951. The locomotive is still in grey primer and had just completed a running in round trip to Manchester. For reasons of simplicity and low cost Riddles chose to construct the 'Britannia' class locomotives (and subsequently all the BR Standard classes with the exception of 71000 DUKE OF GLOUCESTER) as 2-cylinder engines. Riddles subscribed to the belief that 'if all other factors were equal a 2-cylinder steam engine, with 4 beats per revolution, promoted better steaming'.

70008 BLACK PRINCE built Crewe Works, entered service April 1951 with a BR1 4250 gallon/7 ton tender, withdrawn from BR service January 1967. Cut for scrap by Campbells of Airdrie in May/June 1967.

Black Prince, Edward of Woodstock, Prince of Wales, Duke of Cornwall, Prince of Aquitaine, KG (1330–1376) was the eldest son of King Edward III of England and Philippa of Hainault, and father to King Richard II of England. He was an exceptional military leader and his victories over the French first at Crécy and then at Poitiers made him very popular during his lifetime. In 1348 he became the first Knight of the Garter, an order which he helped to found. Edward died one year before his father, becoming the first English born Prince of Wales not to become King of England.

The Standard 'Britannia' class locomotives 6ft 2ins diameter driving wheels (small by accepted express locomotive design practice) can be clearly seen in this image. However, the wheel size was considered large enough for sustained fast running with passenger trains, yet small enough to allow the Britannia class locomotives to be used on freight trains i.e. the 7P (Passenger) 6F (Freight) designations (7P/6F) alternatively referred to as 7MT (Mixed Traffic).

The relatively low axle loading of the class (a little over 20 tons) satisfied BR's intended route availability criteria. In addition, the wheelbase of 58ft 3in meant that the locomotives could be turned on the numerous 60ft turntables then in use around the regions. The classes length over buffers was listed as being 68ft 9in. The first of the class BR No 70000 BRITANNIA was out shopped in unlined black livery which was changed to BR passenger green with black and orange lining, black smoke deflectors smokebox and chimney with a red background to the nameplates and bright metal finish to the wheel rims, handrails, buffers and drawgear prior to the naming ceremony. In traffic the 'Britannia' class livery became BR unlined green without the bright metal fittings.

BR Standard 'Britannia' class 7MT Pacific No 70008 BLACK PRINCE prepares to restart a Norwick–London Liverpool Street service from its Ipswich stop in late November 1960. *John Collins/Rail Photoprints Collection*

70009 ALFRED THE GREAT built Crewe Works, entered service May 1951 with a BR1 4250 gallon/7 ton tender, withdrawn from BR service January 1967. Cut for scrap by McWilliams of Shettlestone in May/June 1967.

Alfred the Great (848/849–899) was King of Wessex from 871 to 899. Born in Wantage then in Berkshire, (now in Oxfordshire) he died in Winchester. Alfred was noted for defending the Anglo-Saxon regions of southern England against the Viking raiders. He is the only English monarch to be accorded the epithet 'the Great' and being the first King of the West Saxons he styled himself overall King of the Anglo Saxons. Reputedly being a man of learning he encouraged education of his subjects, in addition he improved his kingdom's military structure and legal system. Although Alfred was never officially canonized he is regarded a Saint by some members of the Catholic faith whilst the Anglican Communion venerates him as a Christian hero and affords him a feast day on 26 October.

Statue of Alfred the Great in Winchester, unveiled during the millenary commemoration of Alfred's death. *Keith Langston Collection*

BR Standard 'Britannia' class 7MT Pacific No 70009 ALFRED THE GREAT was just one month old when this image was taken at Crewe North shed (5A) on 30 June 1951, the engine is carrying a 70A (Nine Elms) shed plate just prior to being delivered to that depot. The Standard Britannia may well be new but the engine shed roof certainly was not, note the damaged section top right of the image. *Michael Bentley Collection*

70010 OWEN GLENDOWER built Crewe Works, entered service May 1951 with a BR1 4250 gallon/7 ton tender. In 1966 new name plates were fitted taking into account the Welsh spelling of OWAIN GLYNDWR, although the locomotive was withdrawn from BR service in September 1967. Cut for scrap by McWilliams of Shettleston in January 1968.

Owen Glendower (c.1349–c.1416) is William Shakespeare's anglicised version of the Welsh name Owain Glyndŵr or alternatively Owain Glyn Dŵr. He was a Welsh ruler and warrior who was also the last native Welshman to hold the title Prince of Wales. Glyndŵr was a descendant of the Princes of Powys. On 16 September 1400, he instigated the Welsh revolt against the English rule of Henry IV. Although initially successful, the uprising was eventually put down and Glyndŵr, who was last seen publicly in 1412, and was never captured. Details of the final years of his life still remain a mystery. In 2000, celebrations were held all over Wales to commemorate the 600th anniversary of the Glyndŵr rising.

There is a life-size bronze of Wales' 15th Century hero on his battle horse. Set on 8 tons of solid Welsh granite it stands in the Denbighshire town of Corwen. Installed in 2007 it was formally dedicated on 9 November 2009 by Sir Roger Jones. *Keith Langston Collection*

BR Standard 'Britannia' class 7MT Pacific No 70010 OWEN GLENDOWER is seen at Sheffield Victoria station whilst waiting to take over the east bound Manchester–Harwich (Parkstone Quay) train which has just arrived hauled by ex LNER 'B1' class 4-6-0 No 61150 which is stood in the adjacent platform. Note also the young train spotters on the island platform, image taken circa 1959. *Rail Photoprints Collection*

70011 HOTSPUR built Crewe Works, entered service May 1951 with a BR1 4250 gallon/7 ton tender, withdrawn from BR service December 1967. Cut for scrap by McWilliams of Shettleston in March/April 1968.

Hotspur is the nickname of Sir Henry Percy (1364/66–1404) who was also known as Harry Hotspur K.G., he was the eldest son of Henry Percy, 1st Earl of Northumberland, and 4th Lord Percy of Alnwick. The nickname is suggestive of his impulsive nature. Together with his uncle, Thomas Percy, Earl of Worcestershire, he led a rebellion against Henry IV in 1403. Hotspur met his death during defeat at the Battle of Shrewsbury. His remains were first buried at Whitchurch (Salop) but as rumours that he was still alive spread his body was exhumed, cut into quarters, and sent all around the country whilst his severed head was stuck on a pole at the gates of York on the orders of the King. According to popular belief Harry Hotspur has a football club named after him! The Percys owned land in Tottenham Marches between the 17th and 19th centuries, and it is believed that in 1883, when Tottenham Hotspur was named, one of the club's founders read a book about the deeds of knights, when doing so he discovered Hotspur and thought that it would be a name suitable for the football club.

For more information visit www.alnwickcastle.com/whats-on. Alnwick Castle is also home to the Fusiliers Museum.

Hotspurs statue in Alnwick. *Keith Langston Collection*

BR Standard 'Britannia' class 7MT Pacific No 70011 HOTSPUR is seen whilst undergoing its last complete overhaul at Crewe Works on 16 January 1966, just one year and eleven months before it was withdrawn. *Brian Robbins/Rail Photoprints Collection*

70013 OLIVER CROMWELL built Crewe Works, entered service May 1951 with a BR1 4250 gallon/7 ton tender, withdrawn from BR service August 1968. This locomotive is preserved as part of the National Collection. **P**

Oliver Cromwell (1599–1658) was born in Huntingdon, on 25 April 1599 and baptised four days later at the church of St. John. He was the second son of 10 children born to Robert Cromwell and Elizabeth Stewart. He at first attended the free school which was attached to the hospital of St. John in Huntington and later spent a year at Sidney Sussex College, Cambridge.

Following a period of depression and illness during the late 1620s Cromwell was said to have 'experienced a profound spiritual awakening' after which he developed uncompromising Puritan beliefs. With the help of his family connections Cromwell was elected as member of parliament for Huntington in 1628, during that period he became associated with those in opposition to King Charles, and supported the declaration of the Petition of Rights. In 1631 Cromwell's fortunes declined greatly and he experienced leaner times. However, following a substantial inheritance in 1636 he became a freeman of the Borough of Cambridge, and was again elected to Parliament.

During the Civil War Cromwell took up arms for the parliament and was one of the commanders of the New Model Army which defeated the royalists. In addition to his substantial military achievements Cromwell also became known as a strong political leader. He is famously remembered for leading the overthrow of the English monarchy and then turning England into a Republican Commonwealth. After the execution of King Charles in 1649, Cromwell dominated the short-lived Commonwealth of England and also during that period conquered Ireland and Scotland, by his supporters he was widely thought of as being 'King in all but name'.

Cromwell died at Whitehall Palace on 3 September 1658 following a bout of malaria. That night a violent storm swept across England leading Cromwell's enemies to proclaim that the storm was actually a work of the Devil, carrying away the soul of the so called 'Lord Protector'. He was originally buried in Westminster Abbey, however after the Royalists (Stuarts) returned to power, his corpse was dug up, hung in chains, and beheaded. For several decades, the head was displayed spiked on a pole above Westminster Hall. During the 18th/19th centuries Cromwell's head remained a curiosity and as such was often placed on public view. Following scientific analysis in 1960 the head was declared to be 'probably genuine' and was then interred in an undisclosed precise location, but within the chapel of Sidney Sussex College, Cambridge.

BR Standard 'Britannia' class 7MT Pacific No 70013 OLIVER CROMWELL is seen near Wilmslow with a local train on 31 June 1951, this turn was used regularly for a new locomotive running in by Crewe Works. *Gordon Coltas Trust/Mike Bentley Collection*

Preserved BR Standard 'Britannia' class 7MT Pacific No 70013 OLIVER CROMWELL heading a railtour on the WCML at Moore, south of Warrington in April 1968. Note at that time the original nameplates had been removed and replaced by sub-standard looking replicas. *Keith Langston Collection*

Preserved BR Pacific No 70013 OLIVER CROMWELL is seen between mainline charters, on shed at the Carnforth depot of West Coast Railway Company. Carnforth depot was formerly 11A from 1948 until 1958, 24L from April 1958 until September 1963 and thereafter 10A. *Fred Kerr*

BR Pacific No 70013 OLIVER CROMWELL is seen on the turntable at Manchester, Patricroft depot (then 9H) in July 1966. Note that the locomotive's nameplates had already been removed prior to 70013's withdrawal from BR service. *Rail Photoprints Collection*

Preserved BR Pacific No 70013 OLIVER CROMWELL is seen on Cumbrian Mountain Express duty, 11 February 2012, note the modern high intensity light in the centre of the buffer beam. The title Cumbrian Mountain Express was not originally the name of a titled train during the steam era. However, it is an appropriate name created by the post steam era special train/charter industry which has become the well-known popular title of charter trains which use the rail routes within Cumbria (WCML) and also the famous Settle–Carlisle route. *Fred Kerr*

www.youtube.com/watch?v=AreIzpRQFKo
70013 OLIVER CROMWELL attacks the Torbay Banks. The Dartmouth Express, 18 October 2014.

70014 IRON DUKE built Crewe Works, entered service June 1951 with a BR1 4250 gallon/7 ton tender, withdrawn from BR service December 1967. Cut for scrap by Wards of Killamarsh in March/April 1968.

Iron Duke Field Marshal Arthur Wellesley, 1st Duke of Wellington, KG, GCB, GCH, PC, FRS (1769–1852), was an Anglo-Irish soldier and statesman. Wellesley was born in Dublin, Ireland where in 1787 he joined the British Army and first served as aide de camp to two successive Lord Lieutenants of Ireland. He was also a member of the Irish House of Commons. He was a great military leader who participated in over 60 battles, famously defeating Napoleon at the Battle of Waterloo. Wellesley first rose to prominence as a General during the Napoleonic War Peninsular campaign. After leading the allied forces to victory against the French at the Battle of Vitoria he was promoted to the rank of Field Marshal. He served two terms of office as British Prime Minister (1828-1830 and 1834) on both occasions representing the Tory party. He was later sent to the House of Lords where he became 'Leader of the House', he remained Commander in Chief of the British Army until his death at Walmer Castle, Kent at the age of 83.

Wellington's statue in Edinburgh, there is also a statue of him in London adjacent to the Bank of England. *Keith Langston Collection*

BR Britannia Pacific No 70014 IRON DUKE climbs away from Oxenholme with a down express, on 29 July 1967. Note the BR1A tender and that the nameplate has been removed and the name stencilled directly onto the smoke deflectors. *Chris Davies/Rail Photoprints Collection*

70036 BOADICEA built Crewe Works, entered service December 1952 with a BR1 4250 gallon/7 ton tender, withdrawn from BR service October 1966. Cut for scrap by Motherwell Machinery & Scrap of Wishaw in February 1967.

Boudicca statue Westminster London. *Len Mills*

Boadicea, also known as Boudicca (AD60-61) was the Queen of the British Celtic Iceni Tribe who famously led an uprising against the occupying troops of the Roman Empire. The historic events of that time were revived during the English Renaissance and during the Victorian era that led to an increase in the warrior Queen's legendary fame. Queen Victoria was fancifully portrayed as a kindred soul of the so-called Warrior Queen, Boadicea (Boudicca) who has ever since remained a cultural symbol in the UK. The area of London known as Kings Cross was formerly the site of a village called Battle Bridge which marked a crossing of the river Fleet. In the 1930s there was a theory put forward that the Iceni fought a major battle against the Romans in that area. There is a historically unsubstantiated tale suggesting that Boadicea is buried below what in modern times are platforms 9 and 10 of Kings Cross station. However, there is no evidence to support that imaginative story and it is now widely thought to be a post WWII invention.

BR Britannia Pacific No 70036 BOADICEA (note the BR spelling of the name) is seen between turns at Stratford depot (30A) in 1956. *Rail Photoprints Collection*

70037 HEREWARD THE WAKE built Crewe Works, entered service December 1952 with a BR1 4250 gallon/7 ton tender, withdrawn from BR service October 1966. Cut for scrap by McWilliams of Airdrie in February 1968.

Hereward the Wake, who came to be remembered as an English hero, hailed from Bourne in Lincolnshire but was actually of Danish ancestry. The earliest reference to his birth parents declared him the son of Edith (a descendant of Oslac of York) with his father being one Leofric of Bourne. Charles Kingsley in his novel Hereward (1865) portrayed him as the son of Leofric Earl of Mercia, interesting in that if factual his mother could have been none other than Lady Godiva! Living during Saxon times his birth and death dates are uncertain, however he was by all accounts a wilful young man whom King Edward the Confessor saw fit to exile to Europe at the age of 14. At the time of the Norman invasion of England he was still exiled to Europe, where he fought as a mercenary. Hereward returned to England circa 1070 after the defeat of King Harold, and he set about exacting revenge on as many Normans as he could. Hereward discovered that his family's lands had been taken over by the Normans who had killed his brother, placing that man's head on a spike at the gate to his house. Hereward took revenge on the Normans he believed had killed his brother, attacking them whilst they were carousing at a drunken feast. It is alleged that he killed fifteen of them, with the assistance of only one helper. Thereafter with a group of followers he travelled to Peterborough Abbey where he was knighted by his uncle Abbot Brand. He then returned briefly to Flanders to allow the situation to cool down before again returning to England. He was also known as Hereward the Outlaw and Hereward the Exile.

HMS *Hereward* was an H-class destroyer of the Royal Navy commissioned on 9 December 1936. The destroyer was sunk by enemy dive bomber action off Crete on 29 May 1941, 76 crew members lost their lives and the surviving 89 were rescued by the Italian Navy and made prisoners of war.

SC – the letters seen below the cast shedplate indicate that the locomotive is fitted with a 'Self Cleaning' smokebox. Simply explained the SC smokebox was designed to prevent the emission of sparks/hot ash from the chimney. The cleaning effect is achieved by the fitting of vertical diaphragm plates in front of the tube plate and the addition of a horizontal table plate just under the flange of the locomotive's blast pipe, which when set at the correct angle and combined with a wire net screen, caused the hot ashes to be drawn through the wire net screen before being ejected through the chimney. Following that action, the ashes are smaller, practically dead and considered less likely to cause a lineside fire.

BR Britannia Pacific No 70037 HEREWARD THE WAKE is seen moving off after taking water at Huddersfield station in 1960. The locomotive was at that time carrying a March (31B) shedplate. *Rail Photoprints Collection*

70040 CLIVE OF INDIA built Crewe Works, entered service March 1953 with a BR1 4250 gallon/7 ton tender, withdrawn from BR service September 1967. Cut for scrap by McWilliams of Shettleston in November/December 1967.

Clive of India, Major-General Robert Clive, 1st Baron Clive, KB (1725–1774), was a British army officer and soldier of fortune who became British Governor of Bengal.

He is credited with establishing the East India Company in Bengal and together with Warren Hastings he was a key figure in the creation of British India. He was instrumental in establishing the military and political supremacy of the East India Company in Bengal. He is credited with securing a large swathe of South Asia (Bangladesh, India, Pakistan) and securing the wealth gained for the British crown. No mean achievement for a Shropshire born lad who was reportedly expelled from three different schools, he was the eldest son of 13 children.

Clive was perhaps one of the most controversial figures in British military history and is credited with laying the foundations of the British Raj. For his involvement in that act he was vilified, put on trial before parliament when he returned to Britain. Of particular concern was the fact that he had during that period amassed a personal fortune. However, a vote to censure him for his actions failed. Clive was later invested as a member of the Order of the Bath and was appointed to the post of Lord Lieutenant of Shropshire. Additionally, he held an Irish peerage as Baron Clive of Plassey, County Clare. He died in London on 22 November 1774, some say by his own hand during an illness, but that was never conclusively proven. He was buried in St. Margaret's Parish Church at Moreton Say, in Shropshire.

Statue of Clive situated in St. Charles Street, London. There is also a statue of him in the Shropshire town of Shrewsbury. *Keith Langston Collection*

BR Standard 'Britannia' class Pacific No 70040 CLIVE OF INDIA is seen in the shed yard at Patricroft, Manchester in March 1965. The locations shed code was originally 10C from January 1948 to February 1958, thereafter 26F until September 1963, it then became 9H until closure in July 1968. *Rail Photoprints Collection*

70041 SIR JOHN MOORE built Crewe Works, entered service March 1953 with a BR1 4250 gallon/7 ton tender, withdrawn from BR service April 1967. Cut for scrap by McWilliams of Shettleston in September/October1967.

Sir John Moore, Lieutenant-General Sir John Moore, KB (1761–1809) was a celebrated British soldier who also served as a Member of Parliament.

He is remembered for his participation in many military campaigns, for his introduction of military training reforms and for initiating the construction of the Martello Towers on the south coast of England. He was killed during the Battle of Corunna during the Peninsular War and his tomb is situated in San Carlos Garden at La Coruña. Moore was buried wrapped in a military cloak in the ramparts of the town. Moore's funeral was commemorated in the poem 'The Burial of Sir John Moore after Corunna' by Charles Wolfe (1791–1823). Moore was born in Glasgow where his father (also John Moore) was an eminent doctor and writer. Sir John Moore Barracks at Winchester, home of the Army Training Regiment, is named after him. A bronze statue in the form of a monument stands in George Square, Glasgow, additionally there is a monument to him in St. Pauls Cathedral, furthermore 'houses' are named for him at The High School of Glasgow and HM Queen Victoria School, Dunblane.

The Sir John Moore statue located in George Square, Glasgow. *Keith Langston Collection*

BR Standard 'Britannia' class Pacific No 70041 SIR JOHN MOORE is seen at speed passing Winwick, Warrington heading south on the West Coast Main Line (WCML) in this February 1964 image. The BR Standard design high running plate constructed to give easier access to the cylinders and motion is clearly seen. The tender carries the post 1956 'ferret and dartboard' BR crest. *Rail Photoprints Collection*

Lord Roberts, Field Marshal Frederick Sleigh Roberts, 1st Earl Roberts, Bt, VC, KG, KP, GCB, OM, GCSI, GCIE, KStJ, PC (1832–1914) was a distinguished and highly decorated British soldier who was without doubt one of the most successful British commanders of the 19th century. He was born in India and was the second son of Irish born General Sir Abraham Roberts and Edinburgh born Isabella Bunbury. Lord Roberts died of pneumonia whilst visiting WWI troops in France. He was only one of two non-royals to be afforded the privilege of lying in state prior to a state funeral in St. Paul's Cathedral during the 20th century (the other being Sir Winston Churchill). His son Frederick Hugh Sherston Roberts VC was killed in action on 17 December 1899 at the Battle of Colenso, during the Boer War. Roberts and his son were one of only three pairs of fathers and sons to be awarded the Victoria Cross. Today, their Victoria Crosses are displayed in the National Army Museum. Lord Roberts rests within St. Paul's Cathedral. An impressive monument to him in Kelvingrove Park, Glasgow the city of his birth, was unveiled by Lady Roberts in 1914. There is a smaller version of the statue on Horseguards Parade, London and an earlier unveiled original statue was originally erected in North East Calcutta, India (now known as Kolkata).

The Lord Roberts memorial located in Kelvingrove Park, Glasgow. *Keith Langston Collection*

West Coast Main Line (WCML) – Following the British Railways (BR) 1955 modernisation plan the route was upgraded and electrified in stages between 1959 and 1974. The first section to be modernised and electrified was from Crewe to Manchester, completed on 12 September 1960. The Crewe-Liverpool route was the next to be upgraded and that electrification was completed on 1 January 1962. Electrification towards London then began and the first public service with electric trains ran on that section from 18 April 1966, with electrification of the Birmingham line being completed on 6 March 1967. The electrification of the section from Weaver Junction, north to Scotland was completed on 6 May 1974. The system used is 25 kV alternating current (25kv-AC) which is commonly used for railway electrification systems worldwide, and especially for high-speed rail.

BR Standard 'Britannia' class Pacific No 70042 LORD ROBERTS is seen under the wires whilst approaching Winsford with a northbound train for Liverpool during August 1963. *Rail Photo Prints Collection*

70043 LORD KITCHENER built Crewe Works, entered service June 1953 with a BR1 4250 gallon/7 ton tender, withdrawn from BR service August 1965. Cut for scrap by Wards of Beighton in October/November 1965.

Lord Kitchener, Field Marshal Horatio Herbert Kitchener, 1st Earl Kitchener KG, KP, GCB, OM, GCSI, GCMG, GCIE, ADC, PC (1850–1916) was an Irish born highly decorated British soldier who also served in the Cabinet as Secretary of State for War (1914).

His commanding image is remembered to this day from the First World War recruiting poster stating 'Your country needs you!' In 1898 he won fame for securing victory at the Battle of Omdurman in the Sudan, after which he was given the title Lord Kitchener of Khartoum. Kitchener was born in Ballylongford, County Kerry, Republic of Ireland the son of Lt. Col. Henry Horatio Kitchener and Frances Anne Chevallier-Cole.

He died on 5 June 1916 when the warship HMS *Hampshire*, taking him to diplomatic negotiations in Russia, was sunk by a German mine of Marwick Head, Orkney Islands. Kitchener was the most senior officer from either side to die in action during World War One. There is a small squat crenellated tower on the headland at Marwick, which is visible for miles around; neither intended as a castle or lighthouse the structure has no obvious function. However, there is a stone panel which explains, '*This tower was raised by the people of Orkney in memory of Field Marshal Earl Kitchener of Khartoum on that corner of his country which he had served so faithfully nearest to the place where he died on duty. He and his staff perished along with the officers and nearly all the men of* HMS *Hampshire on 5 June, 1916.*'

See also WD 2-10-0 'Austerity' 8F locomotive, Longmoor Military Railway No 601 KITCHENER.

BR Standard 'Britannia' class Pacific No 70043 LORD KITCHENER which was at that time (circa 1957) a Longsight (9A) allocated locomotive is seen at the head of an 8-coach train in an unknown location. *Rail Photoprints Collection*

BR Standard 'Britannia' class Pacific No 70043 LORD KITCHENER is pictured when brand new and ex works at Crewe on 10 May 1953. The sheet of fabric seen emanating from the locomotive cab door is part of a draught excluder screen which was fitted between the engine and tender on later built examples of the class. That modification was made after complaints from locomotive crews, in addition more substantial alterations were later carried out which helped to better address the same problem by improving cab-tender interfaces. *Mike Morant Collection*

This locomotive was one of two members of the 'Britannia' class which were initially fitted with experimental braking equipment, the other being No 70044 EARL HAIG. These locomotives were fitted with Westinghouse airbrake equipment which, as can be seen in this image, was located along either side of the smokebox, and obviously prohibited the fitting of smoke deflectors with the relevant nameplates. The two new locomotives were first delivered to Manchester Longsight depot (9A) in order for a series of brake trials to be carried out with both freight and passenger trains on the London Midland mainline. The predominant trials were reportedly undertaken with 'high speed' mineral (freight) trains comprising of prototype air braked wagons along the London Midland Region's 'Central' line between Toton and Brent. A railway air brake is a power braking system with compressed air as the operating medium. At the conclusion of the trials the two locomotives were returned to the works for the Westinghouse equipment to be removed thereafter smoke deflectors with the appropriate nameplates were fitted.

The Westinghouse Air Brake Company (WABCO) was founded on 28 September 1869 by George Westinghouse in Pittsburgh, Pennsylvania U.S.A. Earlier in the year Westinghouse had invented the railway air brake whilst working at a facility in New York state. After having manufactured equipment in Pittsburgh for a number of years, he began to construct facilities and plants east of the city where homes for his employees were also built. In 1889, the air brake manufacturing facility was moved to Wilmerding, Pennsylvania, and the company's general office building was built there in 1890. WABCO's direct successor companies include WABCO Vehicle Control Systems, a commercial vehicle air brake manufacturer; and WABTEC, a railway equipment manufacturer, which have been owned and operated independently of each other since the mid-twentieth century.

70044 EARL HAIG built Crewe Works, entered service June 1954 with a BR1 4250 gallon/7 ton tender, withdrawn from BR service December 1966. Cut for scrap by Wards of Beighton in February 1967.

Earl Haig, Douglas Haig, 1st Earl Haig, KT, GCB, OM, GCVO, KCIE, ADC, (1861–1928) was a senior British Army officer during World War 1. Haig was commander of the British Expeditionary Force (BEF) from 1915 until the end of the war. He was commander during the Battle of the Somme where the British Army suffered the highest number of battle casualties ever in military history. Haig went on to command the army during the Third Battle of Ypres and the Hundred Days Offensive which followed. He was born in Edinburgh, and his father John Haig was head of the family whisky distilling business Haig & Haig. His name is synonymous with the Haig Fund (more properly entitled the Earl Haig Fund), a charity set up in 1921 to assist ex-servicemen. Today, the Haig Fund continues to support veterans from all conflicts and other military actions involving British Armed Forces up to the present day. Its members sell replica poppies in the weeks before Remembrance Day/Armistice Day, Remembrance Sunday always falls on the second Sunday in November. The words Haig Fund are no longer inscribed on the black button in the centre of each poppy, instead the inscription now reads Poppy Appeal.

BR Standard 'Britannia' class Pacific No 70044 EARL HAIG simmers in the sun at Blackpool South on 2 June 1963. *Ian Turnbull/Rail Photoprints Collection*

BR Standard 'Britannia' class Pacific No 70044 EARL HAIG is seen leaving Manchester London Road station with an up 'The Mancunian' service circa 1959, note the early BR crest on the locomotives tender. 'The Mancunian' Euston-Manchester service first ran on 26 September 1927 and after a break for WWII the headboard was reintroduced on 26 September 1949 and this titled train last ran on 15 April 1966. London Road station opened as Store Street in 1842 and was renamed Manchester London Road in 1847. After being rebuilt in 1960 it became Manchester Piccadilly. The station serves intercity destinations such as London (Euston), Birmingham, Bristol, Southampton, South Wales and Glasgow as well as other destinations throughout Northern England including Liverpool, Leeds, Sheffield, Newcastle and York. *Rail Photoprints Collection*

BR Standard 'Britannia' class Pacific No 70044 EARL HAIG is seen shortly after passing Winsford on the West Coast Main Line (WCML) with an up express in August 1963. *Rail Photoprints Collection*

70045 LORD ROWALLAN built Crewe Works, entered service June 1954 with a BR1D 4725 gallon/9 ton tender with steam powered coal pusher, withdrawn from BR service December 1967. Cut for scrap by Wards of Beighton in February/March 1968.

Lord Rowallan, Thomas Godfrey Olson Corbett, 2nd Baron Rowallan, KT, KBE, MC, TD (1895–1977) was a senior British Army officer. Born in Chelsea he was also the first son of property developer, and Liberal Politician Archibald Corbett and Alice Mary Polson.

He served with distinction in both World Wars and attained the rank of Lieutenant Colonel. At Boyelles on 30 March 1918, Corbett attempted to dig out some wounded soldiers who had been buried by artillery action, whilst 'under heavy fire and in full view of the enemy.' In doing so he received a leg wound which left him with a permanent disability, for that act he was awarded the Military Cross. In 1939 he raised a new Territorial Army battalion of the Royal Scots Fusiliers with whom he served in France as part of the British Expeditionary Force (BEF). On being demobilized from the army in 1944 he took up the post of Chief Scout of the British Commonwealth and Empire in 1945 and also served for a period as *Governor of Tasmania*. Rowallan Power Station in north-western Tasmania, which came into use in 1967, and its associated lake are named in his honour. As Chief Scout, Rowallan travelled widely in the Commonwealth and other countries, encouraging the post-war growth of scouting. Rowallan served on the World Scout Committee of the movement from 1947 until 1953. During that period, he was also a governor of the National Bank of Scotland. Lord Rowallan died at Rowallan Castle, Kilmarnock on 30 November 1977.

BR Standard 'Britannia' class Pacific No 70045 LORD ROWALLAN is seen at Carlisle Upperby shed (then 12B) in the company of an ex LMS locomotive with a military name, re-built Royal Scot No 46103 ROYAL SCOTS FUSILER a Carlisle allocated locomotive. At that time, No 70045 was allocated to Aston depot (21D). *Rail Photoprints Collection*

During the BR era, the station carried the name Leeds City. However, after an extensive 1967 rebuild and the closure of other local stations the former LNWR/NER joint station (often previously referred to as the 'New' station) was simply called Leeds.

The 1962 built high rise building seen in this image is in modern times referred to as City House. Designed by the infamous architect John Poulson it was originally called British Railways House. The poet John Betjeman publicly criticised the design which he claimed 'blocked all the light out of City Square and was only a testament to money, having no architectural merit'.

In 2011 Leeds City Council granted planning permission for the external and internal refurbishment of the building.

70046 ANZAC built Crewe Works, entered service June 1954 with a BR1D 4725 gallon/9 ton tender with steam powered coal pusher, withdrawn from BR service July 1967. Cut for scrap by Campbells of Airdrie between December 1967 and January 1968.

Anzac, the Australian and New Zealand Army Corps. Initially this acronym was used to describe a First World War Mediterranean Expeditionary Force that was formed in Egypt during 1915, and which fought with great distinction during the Battle of Gallipoli. The corps was officially disbanded in 1916 following the allied evacuation of the Gallipoli peninsular and the subsequent formation of the 1st and 2nd Anzac Corps. Over time Anzac became the term used to describe any military formation containing Australian and/or New Zealand units. Anzac Day is a national day of remembrance in both Australia and New Zealand, which is commemorated annually on 25 April.

Two Anzac Memorials featuring bronze sculptures of Australian and New Zealand soldiers on plinths, are located at the western approach of the Anzac Bridge at Rozelle, Sydney. The sculpture of an Australian ANZAC soldier facing west was unveiled on ANZAC Day in 2000. *L Johnson*

BR Standard 'Britannia' class Pacific No 70046 ANZAC is seen on shed at Willesden (1A) on 11 August 1963, although almost four years before its withdrawn date the locomotive is already without nameplates. At that time, No 70046 was allocated to Holyhead (6J). No doubt modern day Health & Safety would have had something adverse to say about the trackside clutter! *Rail Photoprints Collection*

BR Standard 'Britannia' class Pacific No 70046 ANZAC arrives at Tamworth Low Level with a WCML Euston–Manchester service, circa 1960. Note Tamworth High Lever station (Birmingham–Derby route) of which a portion straddles the overbridge, the large timber framed structure was one of the lift shafts built to aid the transfer of mail between the higher and lower two sets of platforms. The railways traditionally played a large part in the regional distribution of mail, a practice which continued during the British Railways era. *Rail Photoprints Collection*

BR Standard 'Britannia' class Pacific No 70046 ANZAC (then minus nameplates) speeds past Winwick with a northbound WCML express in April 1965. *Rail Photoprints Collection*

70048 THE TERRITORIAL ARMY, 1908–1958, built Crewe Works, entered service July 1954 with a BR1D 4725 gallon/9 ton tender with steam powered coal pusher. This locomotive originally entered BR service unnamed, being subsequently named on 23 July 1958. Withdrawn from BR service May 1967. Cut for scrap by McWilliams of Shettleston between September and October 1967.

The Territorial Army, or TA as it is commonly referred to, is part of the UK's reserve land forces, which provides support to the regular army at home and overseas, and is the largest of all the UK's reserve forces. Now known as the Army Reserve it fits within the make-up of the greater British Army. The other reserve forces being the Royal Naval Reserve (RNR), the Royal Marines Reserve (RMR) and the Royal Air Force Volunteer Reserve (RAFVR). The Army Reserve provides support to the Regular Army at home and overseas, and throughout its history almost every major military operation has seen reservists operate alongside their Regular Army counterparts.

The first TA units were stood up on 1 April 1908, and that date is accepted as the birth of what we know today as the Territorial Army. The Territorial Force was subsequently mobilised in August 1914, its soldiers fighting alongside, and indistinguishable from the Regular Army. Upon demobilisation in 1918 Territorial Force units were disbanded, but were reconstituted in 1920 as the part-time Territorial Army. Upon the outbreak of hostilities in September 1939, the Territorial Army was again mobilised. When the Army again demobilised in 1946 the TA was temporarily suspended, but was reconstituted in 1947 as a part-time reservist force. In 2004 the Government announced a radical restructuring of the Army, leading to the realignment of the TA as reservists of the regular regiments. Under TA Rebalancing, 15 TA infantry battalions were reduced to 14, but reportedly the overall strength of the force remained the same.

BR Standard 'Britannia' class Pacific No 70048 THE TERRITORIAL ARMY, 1908–1958 is seen passing Gloucester Eastgate station in November 1962. Note the Willesden shed plate (1A) and the huge pile of coal over the platform beyond the front of the locomotive. *Rail Photoprint Collection*

On 8 November 2008, preserved sister Britannia Pacific No 70013 OLIVER CROMWELL temporarily carried the original TERRITORIAL ARMY 1908–1958 nameplate on one side of the locomotive (silver letters on red background) as part of the 100th anniversary celebration of the TA. The locomotive is seen hard at work with a recreation freight train at the Great Central Railway (GCR). The commemorative temporary re-naming was carried out by HRH The Duke of Gloucester. In October 2016, a nameplate from the locomotive sold at auction for £9,800. *Fred Kerr*

BR Standard Britannia class Pacific No 70048 THE TERRITORIAL ARMY 1908–1958 awaits departure from Euston station with a down express for Glasgow 30 July 1964. At that time, comprehensive reconstruction of the station was underway. *Chris Davies/Rail Photoprints*

Class Details

'Britannia Class' BR Standard Pacific 7P6F Classification	4-6-2	55 built 1951–1954 at Crewe Works	Driving Wheel 6ft 2ins dia.	2 – cylinders Walschaert piston valves	Working BP 250psi Superheated Tractive effort 32160lbf

Two 'Britannia' class locomotives are preserved and both have been used regularly hauling charter/special trains in many locations on the national rail network.

BR No 70000 BRITANNIA was in 2017 owned and operated by the Royal Scot Locomotive and General Trust. For more information visit www.iconsofsteam.com/locos/britannia/

BR No 70013 OLIVER CROMWELL was in 2017 owned and operated as part of the National Railway Museum's collection. For more information visit www.nrm.org.uk/

'Britannia' class Pacific No 70000 BRITANNIA is seen at the Nene Valley Railway hauling a rake of Continental coaching stock in September 1981. *Rail Photoprints Collection*

BR Standard 'Britannia' class Pacific No 70013 OLIVER CROMWELL was pictured at Newton Heath depot (9D) just prior to being withdrawn for preservation. Note that the name and smokebox number plate have been removed for safe keeping and that the locomotive carries a hand painted 12A shedplate (Carlisle Kingmore). *Keith Langston Collection*

Newly refurbished and re-painted preserved BR Standard 'Britannia' class Pacific No 70000 BRITANNIA is seen under test at LNWR Crewe during January 2012. *Keith Langston Collection*

Chapter 5

WAR DEPARTMENT AUSTERITY LOCOMOTIVES INCLUDING LONGMOOR MILITARY RAILWAY (LMR)

MOS 'WD' 8F Austerity 2-10-0

Ministry of Supply 'War Department' Austerity 2-10-0 locomotives AD600 GORDON and AD601 KITCHENER stand alongside each other in the locomotive depot at the former Longmoor Military Railway (LMR). GORDON is taking water whilst KITCHENER is no longer in use. In this image, it can be seen that No AD601 had been roughly painted green over its usual LMR blue livery following the locomotives role in the opening credits of the film 'The Great St. Trinian's Train Robbery', in keeping with that it carried a fake BR smokebox number. After the Longmoor Railway closed an attempt was made to establish a preservation centre on the site, but sadly it failed due to adverse local pressure. This image was taken on Saturday 30 April 1966. *Geoff Plumb*

To see other images in the Geoff Plumb collection, visit https://plumbloco.smugmug.com/

MoS 'WD' 8F 2-10-0 KICHENER, built North British Locomotive Co. Ltd, Hyde Park Works, Glasgow to the order number L948 which was placed on 30 March 1944. The 2-10-0 went into Military service during 1945 as No 73797. 'WD' 8F No 73797 was loaned to British Railways (BR) between 1957 and 1959. Thereafter the Riddles Austerity 2-10-0 returned to the Longmoor Military Railway and was re-numbered 601 (AD601). For a period in service the locomotive was converted to an oil burner accordingly it was reportedly at Eastleigh Works during 1963, for various repairs which included the fitting of a new oil burner in the firebox. Withdrawn by the LMR in 1968 and scrapped shortly afterwards. (The LMR closed in 1969).

Lord Kitchener, Field Marshall Horatio Herbert Kitchener, 1st Earl Kitchener KG, KP, GCB, OM, GCSI, GCMG, GCIE, ADC, PC (1850-1916) was an Irish born highly decorated British soldier who also served in the Cabinet as Secretary of State for War (1914). See also BR 'Britannia' class Pacific No 70043 LORD KITCHENER.

The name KITCHENER was also carried by LMR 0-6-0ST No 70208 a Bagnall 1938 built engine (works No 2587) taken out of service in 1947.

In 1943 the Ministry of Supply ordered 150 Riddles designed 2-10-0 freight locomotives which were all built by the North British Locomotive Co, Glasgow. After the cessation of hostilities 25 of the class were loaned to British Railways (BR) at Nationalisation in January 1948 and purchased by BR at the end of that year, running mainly in Scotland. Their MoD Nos 73774–73796 and 73799, they were latter allotted the BR running numbers 90750–90774 (1961–1962). Additionally, BR took on temporary loan locomotive No 601 KITCHENER (WD No 73797) from the Longmoor Military Railway (LMR), during the period 1957 to 1959. Amongst those examples of the class which returned to the LMR after war service was locomotive No 600 GORDON, WD No 73651 (never taken into BR stock) which is preserved and based at the Severn Valley Railway (SVR). The class was effectively an enlarged version of the WD 2-8-0 Austerity '8F' locomotives but with an extra set of wheels and wider steel fireboxes (3 arch tubes for easy conversion to oil firing).

They were built as 2-10-0s in order to enable them to more easily work over lightly laid track (wartime and occupation conditions). With the exception of the solitary Midland 0-10-0 'Lickey Banker' they were the first successful locomotives with 10 coupled wheels to work in the UK (post Grouping). The middle driving wheels of the class have no flange, to ease turning on tighter tracks. They were the forerunners of the famous Riddles BR Standard '9F' 2-10-0 locomotives built between 1954-1960.

Of the 150 locomotives built all but No 73651 and Nos 73774–73799 were sent overseas. In 1944 20 were dispatched to the Middle East, others were ferried to Europe and in 1944/45 there were reportedly 43 in Belgium and 60 in Holland, but by June 1946 all of those (103 engines) were relocated into Holland. Before being delivered to the military authorities the 2-10-0s were observed 'running in' on the national network where they aroused a good deal of interest amongst the railway fraternity.

There are four preserved examples of the class but none of those were ever taken into stock by British Railways. However, only one of those worked in the UK prior to preservation, that being Longmoor Military Railway (LMR) No 600 GORDON which in addition to being in regular service on the LMR did haul special trains on the mainline. Although the 2-10-0 design was primarily intended for overseas use, 'GORDON' never saw wartime service outside the UK.

The nameplate, regimental crest and NBL works plate of preserved LMR 'WD' 2-10-0 8F locomotive No 600 GORDON, seen in the engine house at the Severn Valley Railway (SVR). Note the flangeless centre driving wheel. *Keith Langston Collection*

However, during the 1957 Suez crisis the WD locomotive reportedly worked highly secretive trains between the Longmoor military base and Southampton. GORDON was the second of the class to enter service and had the distinction of being the last steam locomotive owned by the British Army. After WWII, the locomotive remained at Longmoor and was eventually transferred to the SVR in 1972. In May 1980 No 600 took part in the parade of locomotives at 'Rocket 150', the 150th anniversary of the opening of the Liverpool & Manchester Railway held at Rainhill. On 25 July 2008, the then 'on loan' WD Austerity 2-10-0 was formally handed over to the SVR by the British Army. In 2017 the WD 2-10-0 was a static exhibit in the 'Engine House' at the SVR, whilst awaiting a possible overhaul.

For additional information visit www.svr.co.uk/enginehouse.aspx

---

MoS 'WD' 8F 2-10-0 No 3651 (73651) later becoming Longmoor Military Railway (LMR) No AD600 **GORDON** (SVR No 600), built North British Locomotive Co. Ltd, Hyde Park Works, Glasgow, works number 25437. Into service 1943. **P**

WD No 70205 also carried the name GORDON. It is the last surviving Welsh standard-gauge locomotive, ex Taff Vale Railway 'O1' class No 28 which was purchased by Longmoor Military Railway (LMR) in 1927 and later sold to South Hetton Colliery, County Durham in 1947. Now preserved as part of the National Collection (NRM).

Statue of Gordon in Gravesend, Kent. *Len Mills*

Major General Charles George Gordon CB (28 January 1833–26 January 1885), also known as Chinese Gordon, Gordon Pasha, and Gordon of Khartoum, was a British Army officer and administrator. He was the son of a senior army officer and was commissioned into the Royal Engineers in 1852. Having seen action with the British Army during the Crimean War (1853–1856) Gordon travelled to China and his exploits in that country earned him an impressive military reputation. He commanded the Chinese 'Ever Victorious Army', a force of Chinese soldiers led by European officers. That force was instrumental in putting down the 'Taiping Rebellion', often fighting successfully against overwhelming odds. It was those accomplishments which gained him the title Chinese Gordon and earned him honours from both the Chinese and British governments. Gordon returned to the Sudan during 1873, and with British Government approval, he entered the service of the Khedive (that title being Otterman Turkish in origin and indicating a social standing equivalent to Viceroy). Gordon went on to become Governor-General of the Sudan and in that capacity, he did much to suppress revolts and hamper the slave trade. Declaring himself to be 'exhausted' he resigned that post in 1880 and returned to Europe.

In 1884 a serious revolt broke out in the Sudan, led by the self-proclaimed 'Mahdi, Muhammad Ahmad' a Muslim leader. As a consequence of which Gordon was sent to Khartoum with orders to secure the evacuation of British civilians and loyal members of the army, and thereafter depart with them. He successfully evacuated some 2,500 civilians to safety but in direct contravention of his orders he then chose to stay on with a small band of soldiers and non-military personnel.

Khartoum was besieged by the Mahdi's forces and for almost a year Gordon's city-wide defence held out. During the siege, Gordon and the Mahdi corresponded, each of the men unsuccessfully attempting to convert the other to his faith. The British public admired Gordon for his stoic defence of the city but that admiration was not shared by the government, who would have preferred him not to have got entrenched in the first place. Only when the government was put under public pressure did they react and finally send a relief force. It arrived two days after Khartoum had fallen and Gordon had been killed.

SVR 'WD' Austerity 2-10-0 locomotive LMR No 600 GORDON is seen on shed at Bridgnorth in blue Longmoor Military Railway (LMR) livery. The Riddles designed 'WD' 8F has been out of service since 2005. *Keith Langston Collection*

MoS 'WD' 8F 2-10-0 No 3755 (73755) ex WD 73651 built North British Locomotive Co. Ltd, Hyde Park Works, Glasgow, works number 25601. Into service 1945. Later becoming Dutch State Railways No 5085 **LONGMOOR. P**

LONGMOOR is on static display at the Nederlands Spoorwegmuseum (Dutch Railway Museum) in Utrecht. That example became the 1000th British built steam locomotive to be shipped to mainland Europe in support of the British Army, and the specially cast name plate records that fact. After the war, 'WD' No 73755 became one of several ex-WD locomotives sold to Dutch State Railways (NS). The Riddles 2-10-0 was withdrawn in 1952 and stored pending preservation.

Longmoor Military Railway (LMR) was a British military railway in Hampshire, built by the Royal Engineers from 1903 onwards in order to train army personnel on railway construction and operations. The site was initially known as the Woolmer Instructional Military Railway. Originally a narrow-gauge system the railway was re-laid to standard-gauge between 1905–1907. It was renamed the Longmoor Military Railway in 1935. In the late 1960s, and in light of the reducing role of the military and the severely reduced British Empire, it was decided by the Ministry of Defence to close the railway. Preservation groups became interested in acquiring complete LMR system, and a bid was placed to purchase the site along with the airstrip at Gypsy Hollow which would have enabled the production of a unique transport museum. The MOD rejected this proposal, which had been backed by the Association of Railway Preservation Societies and The Transport Trust. The last day of operation was 31 October 1969 and the railway was completely closed in 1971.

www.youtube.com/watch?v=da1CbHWAqQo
Farewell to the Longmoor Military Railway.

SVR 'WD' Austerity 2-10-0 locomotive LMR No 600 GORDON is seen on passing Rifle Range on the SVR with a Bridgnorth-Kidderminster train on 17 August 1997. *Fred Kerr*

MoS 'WD' 8F 2-10-0 BR No 90775 (fictitious number the last of the class carried BR No 90774). Built by the North British Locomotive Company in 1943 MoD No 3652 (76352) Hellenic State Railways No Lb951. This locomotive was repatriated from Greece direct to the North Norfolk Railway (2006), and never worked for BR. Has carried the name **STURDIE** as LMR No 601. **P**

Lieutenant General Sir Vernon Ashton Hobart Sturdee, KBE, CB, DSO.

In 2017 the Riddles Austerity freight locomotive was out of service and under overhaul at the North Norfolk Railway. For more information www.nnrailway.co.uk/steamlocos. php

Lieutenant General Sir Vernon Ashton Hobart Sturdee, KBE, CB, DSO (1890–1966) was an Australian Army commander who served two terms as Chief of the General Staff.

A regular officer of the Royal Australian Engineers who joined the Militia in 1908, he was one of the original Anzacs during WW1, participating in the landing at Gallipoli on 25 April 1915. At the onset of WWII, he held the rank of colonel becoming a lieutenant general in 1940, he later became Chief of the General Staff. In 1942, he became head of the Australian Military Mission to Washington, D.C. As commander of the First Army in New Guinea in 1944–45, Sturdee directed the fighting at Aitape, and also on New Britain and Bougainville. When the war ended, Sturdee took the surrender of Japanese forces in the Rabaul area. As one of the Army's most senior officers, he became Commander in Chief of the Australian Military Forces in December 1945. He then became the Chief of the General Staff for a second time in 1946, serving in that post until his retirement in 1950.

MoS 'WD' 8F 2-10-0 No 3672 (73672). Built by the North British Locomotive Company in 1944 works No 25458. The locomotive was shipped to Egypt but by October 1945 it was declared surplus to requirements and sold to the Hellenic State Railways (Greece) and re-numbered Lb960, working on express passenger services in the Salonika district. Withdrawn in 1979 this WD 2-10-0 never worked for BR. In August 1984, the locomotive was repatriated from Greece direct to the UK. No name carried in service but named **DAME VERA LYNN** in preservation. **P**

'Forces Sweetheart' Vera Lynn sings at a munitions factory in 1941.

After a period in store the locomotive was purchased by a group of Mid-Hants Railway (MHR) members and shipped to the UK. It was then bought by Mr D. Milham for use on his Lavender Line, East Sussex. After some preliminary repairs the locomotive was named on 6 August 1985 by the 'Dame' herself and thereafter steamed for a short period at the aforementioned line. In 1986 it was bought by Clifford Brown, a British-born businessman living in Virginia, U.S.A. After visiting several British preserved railways, Mr. Brown decided that he wished the locomotive to be based on the North Yorkshire Moors Railway (NYMR), and it arrived there in December 1986. In 1998 the locomotive was taken out of service and in 2017 the privately owned MoS 'WD' 2-10-0 was awaiting an overhaul at the NYMR.

For more information visit http://www.dameveralynn.co.uk/

Dame Vera Margaret Lynn CH DBE OStJ (née Welch; born 20 March 1917), widely known as 'the Forces' Sweetheart', is a British singer, songwriter, and actress whose musical recordings and performances were enormously popular during the Second World War. During the war she toured Egypt, India, giving outdoor concerts for the troops in addition to entertaining munition workers etc. The songs most associated with her are 'We'll Meet Again', 'The White Cliffs of Dover', 'A Nightingale Sang in Berkeley Square' and 'There'll Always Be an England'. She has devoted much time and energy to charity work connected with ex-servicemen, disabled children, and breast cancer. She is still held in great affection by old soldiers of WWII and all who lived through that era.

Preserved 'WD' Austerity 2-10-0 NBL No 25458 (WD 3672–73672) DAME VERA LYNN is seen at Grosmont station NYMR on 24 August 1994. *Fred Kerr*

MOS 'WD' 8F Austerity 2-8-0

None of this large British Railways class (Nos 90000-90732) have been preserved, but one locomotive from the batch that worked overseas is now based in the UK. Vulcan Foundry 1945 built 'WD' 9257 (79257) was shipped to Holland and after the war it first became Dutch State Railway No 4464 before in 1952 being bought by Swedish State Railway, becoming that railways No 1931. After being withdrawn (October 1956) it was stored out of use as part of Sweden's Strategic Reserve until 1972. It was brought back to the UK in 1973 (KWVR). The locomotive was in service until 1976 when it was withdrawn to facilitate a general overhaul and the building of a new tender. The engine re-entered service at the Keighley & Worth Valley Railway (KWVR) on 23 July 2007 with the fictitious BR No 90733 (one number later than the last BR class member), and is 2017 the 2-8-0 was reportedly available for service.

See also kwvr.co.uk/steam-train/war-department-wd-austerity-2-8-0-90733/
https://www.youtube.com/watch?v=Pb6q4d8RT4A ('WD' 2-8-0 No 90773 at the KWVR).

Two locomotives from the 'WD' owned batch of Riddles Austerity 2-8-0 freight locomotives were retained for service on the Longmoor Military Railway in Hampshire (LMR). Either or both of those locomotives may have occasionally ventured onto BR tracks but they mainly worked on the LMR system. The Austerity 2-8-0 design was developed from the highly successful Stanier 8F which was when first introduced (1943) referred to as the 'the standard type for war work'. The Riddles Austerity 2-8-0 class was developed because it was thought that a similar design to the aforementioned Stanier locomotive was needed but because of war time constraints it would have to be produced at a lower cost. The class was only intended for short term war service. Many Austerity 2-8-0s saw service in France, Holland and Belgium during WWII.

Preserved 'WD' 2-8-0 No 90773 at Haworth locomotive depot KWVR. *Andrew Hastie*

In total 934 'WD' Austerity 2-8-0 locomotives were built at the North British Locomotive Company, Glasgow and Vulcan Foundry, Newton-le-Willows between 1943 and 1946. The Riddles design was developed from the highly successful Stanier '8F' freight locomotive class. The design was developed at minimal cost and many of the locomotives saw service overseas during WWII. British Railways listed 733 of the class in their 1949 stock. The North British locomotives numbered by BR 90000–90421 and the Vulcan Foundry locomotives BR 90422–90732.

Newly built 'WD' 2-8-0 No 7050 is seen alongside the mainline and adjacent to Vulcan Bank Signal Box. No 7050 later became No 77050 and in December 1948 BR No 90521, which was scrapped in January 1965. Many locomotive builders were also involved in the production of munitions; accordingly, the locomotive is seen in the company of a Vulcan Foundry built tank known jointly as the 'Infantry Tank II' and the 'Matilda II', both delivered during May 1943. The 'Matilda II' tanks served for the duration of the war and was always associated with the North Africa Campaign. *Keith Langston Collection*

General Sir Guy Charles Williams KCB CMG DSO (1881–1959) was a British Army General during World War II. Guy Williams was commissioned into the Royal Engineers and served in World War 1. In 1923 he was appointed Deputy Military Secretary at the War Office and then as Commander of 8th Brigade in 1927, in 1928 he became Engineer in Chief at Aldershot Command. In 1934 he moved to the Staff College in Quetta, India serving as Commandant until 1937 when he became General Officer Commanding 5th Division. He served in WW II as General Officer Commander-in-Chief Eastern Command from 1938 to 1941 when he was appointed Military Adviser to the New Zealand Government: he retired later that year.

This sorry sight in the Longmoor Military Railway's shed yard during a public open day on 30 April 1966 depicts 'WD' 2-8-0 LMR No 400 SIR GUY WILLIAMS with what looks like a firebox that's been opened like a can of beans! One of the personnel based at Longmoor at that time, 'Lofty' Ailwood, has stated that: 'This loco opened a crack between the washout plugs top right hand side of the boiler on a down passenger train. Her crew bailed out the fire, and opened the cladding to see the extent of the problem.' No 400 was built by the North British Locomotive Company (NBL) in 1943, Works No 25205. *Mike Morant Collection*

In all military conflicts the skills of engineers have proved invaluable. Simply put, without engineers there would have been no supply to the armies, because the Royal Engineers (REs) maintained the railways, roads, water supplies, bridges and battlefield transport vehicles and links. In many theatres of war the REs also operated the railways and inland waterways. They also installed and maintained the telephones, wireless and other essential items of signalling equipment. The REs often designed and built fortifications in addition to maintaining guns and other weapons.

Cap badge of the Royal Engineers.

Hants & Surrey Tour 26 September 1953. This was the first railtour charted by the Railway Enthusiasts Club at Farnborough and apparently started at North Camp. The motive power for much of the tour was provided by Drummond 'L12' BR No 30434 hauling LSWR pull-push set No 348. However, having traversed the Bordon branch the tour then proceeded to Longmoor Downs on the military railway behind the LMR's 'WD' 2-8-0 LMR No 401 MAJOR GENERAL MCMULLEN which is depicted awaiting departure for Bordon. *Mike Morant collection*

MoS 'WD' 8F 2-8-0 No 79250. Built by Vulcan Foundry in 1945 works No 5193. The locomotive was re-numbered in the 'WD' 1957 listings as LMR No 401 and named **MAJOR GENERAL McMULLEN**, scrapped 1957.

Major-General Sir Donald Jay McMullen CB KBE DSO (1891–12 November 1967) was a British Army officer serving with the Royal Engineers. He served in both of the World Wars. During his military career, he had a long-standing association with railways and locomotives. He was a staff Captain in the Mechanical Depot Branch of the War Office during 1914/15. From 1915 to 1919 he served with the Royal Engineers on the Mudros Light Railway (Gallipoli), the Suez Canal Military Railway, the Kaulara Military Railway (India) and also as Locomotive Superintendent of the Palestine Light Railway.

'WD' Austerity 2-8-0 No 7074 is seen outside Vulcan Works when newly built in July 1943, this locomotive later became WD No 77074 and then BR No 90543 in December 1948, it was scrapped in August 1965. *Keith Langston Collection*

'WD' Austerity 2-8-0 BR No 90513 is pictured in the late 1960s whilst working a heavy freight train over the Blackford Hill section of the Edinburgh Suburban Line. This locomotive was built by Vulcan Foundry and entered service in January 1945 and was formerly No 3192 and LNER No 63192, withdrawn by BR in July 1962 and cut up in the September of that year. *David Anderson*

Class Details

'WD' Austerity Class 8F Classification	2-8-0	934 built 1943-1946 North British Locomotive and Vulcan Foundry	Driving Wheel 4ft 8 ½ ins dia.	2 – cylinders Walschaert piston valves	Working BP 250psi Superheated Tractive effort 34,215 flb
'WD' Austerity Class 8F Classification	2-10-0	150 built 1943 North British Locomotive	Driving Wheel 4ft 8 ½ ins dia.	2 – cylinders Walschaert piston valves	Working BP 250psi Superheated Tractive effort 34,215 flb

MOS 'WD' Austerity 0-6-0 Saddle Tank

The Longmoor Military Railway (LMR) operated a large selection of locomotives during its illustrious history, and many of those carried appropriate names. The names were often swapped between different locomotives as they were taken in and out of service. In addition to the 2-8-0 and 2-10-0 freight locomotives, Riddles (in conjunction with the Hunslet Engine Company) also designed for the Ministry of Supply (WD) a large class of powerful 0-6-0ST (Saddle Tank) engines (BR-E 'J94' class). The locomotives were built between 1943 and 1946 by Hudswell-Clarke, Bagnall, Robert Stephenson & Hawthorn, Hunslet Engine Company, Barclay and Vulcan Foundry. With the look of a traditional industrial shunting locomotive the inside cylinder 'J94' class was British Railways power rated at 4F and had 4ft 3 ins diameter driving wheels, BR listed 75 of the class in 1949. In the region of 70 examples of the class found their way into preservation and the 'J94's are thus said to be the largest class in preservation, with many carrying names. The list of preserved ex War Department 0-6-0ST locomotives includes the following examples with military associated names.

See also https://en.wikipedia.org/wiki/Longmoor_Military_Railway#Locomotives

> **MOS 'WD' Austerity 0-6-0 Saddle Tank**, 1943 Hunslet Engine Co built works number 2857, WD No 75008 SWIFTSURE. In 2017 this locomotive was listed as operational by its home base the East Lancashire Railway (ELR). **P**

For more information visit www.eastlancsrailway.org.uk/

Preserved Austerity 0-6-0ST 'WD' No 75008 SWIFTSURE is seen at Bury Bolton Street station ELR in April 2005. *Mike Buck*

Swiftsure. The Swiftsure name was given to a class of 6 nuclear-powered submarines in service with the Royal Navy from the early 1970s until 2010. They were built by Vickers Shipbuilding & Engineering Ltd, Barrow in Furness and commissioned between 1973 and 2010. One of the class also carried the name HMS *SWIFTSURE*, and that vessel was commissioned in 1973 and de-commissioned in 1992. There was also a 'Swiftsure' class of two British battleships one of which was also named HMS *SWIFTSURE* and launched by Armstrong Whitworth, Elswick in 1903 and decommissioned circa 1920. The other vessel was named HMS *TRIUMPH* and launched by Vickers Sons & Maxim, Barrow in Furness also in 1903, that battleship was sunk by a *U-21* in May 1915 during that action 78 crew members sadly lost their lives. The ships were originally intended for use by the Chilean Navy.

MOS 'WD' Austerity 0-6-0 Saddle Tank, 1944 Hunslet Engine Co built works number 3163, 'WD' No 75113 and 132 SAPPER. In 2016/17 this privately-owned locomotive was listed as operational by the Avon Valley Railway (AVR). **P**

For more information visit www.avonvalleyrailway.org/

Sapper. A sapper, is a term used by the British Army, Commonwealth nations, Polish Army and US Military. Sappers are also referred to as pioneers or combat engineers. The phrase 'sapper' comes from the French *saper*, meaning to undermine, to dig under a wall or building to cause its collapse. They are also trained to serve as infantry personnel in both defensive and offensive operations. In addition to laying and clearing minefields Sappers also carry out such tasks as bridge building, road building and airfield construction and repair. In short, their duties are devoted to facilitating movement, defence and survival of allied forces whilst impeding those of the enemy. British infantry regiments still maintain assault pioneer units. See also ROYAL PIONEER on the following page.

Preserved Austerity 0-6-0ST 'WD' No 75113 (132) SAPPER with 'WD' Green livery is seen with a brake van whilst approaching Middle Forge Junction on the Dean Forest Railway (DFR) in April 2011. This ex WD/LMR locomotive was previously based at the South Devon Railway. In 2009 it was sold to a private buyer and refurbished 2010/2011. *Adam Williams*

For more information visit http://www.norfolksteamloco.co.uk/

MOS 'WD' Austerity 0-6-0 Saddle Tank, 1944 Hunslet Engine Co built works number 3193,' WD' No 75142 and 140 NORFOLK REGIMENT. In 2016/17 this locomotive was reported as being under overhaul at the site of Norfolk Heritage Steam Railway Ltd. **P**

Norfolk Regiment. The Royal Norfolk Regiment was a line infantry regiment of the British Army until 1959. Its predecessor regiment was raised in 1685 as Henry Cornewall's Regiment of Foot. In 1751, it was numbered like most other Army regiments and named the 9th Regiment of Foot. It was formed as the Norfolk Regiment in 1881 under the Childers Reforms of the British Army, as the county regiment of Norfolk by merging the 9th (East Norfolk) Regiment of Foot with the local Militia and Rifle Volunteers battalions. The regiment fought with distinction in both World Wars. In 1959 the Royal Norfolk Regiment was amalgamated as part of the reorganisation of the British Army resulting from the 1957 Defence White Paper becoming part of a new formation, the 1st East Anglian Regiment, part of the East Anglian Brigade.

For more information visit www.royalnorfolkregimentalmuseum.org.uk/

MOS 'WD' Austerity 0-6-0 Saddle Tank, 1944 Robert Stephenson & Hawthorn built works number 7136, 'WD' No 75186 and 150 **ROYAL PIONEER**. In 2016/17 this locomotive was reported as being under overhaul at the site of Peak Rail. Has run in preservation as BR 68013 which was a former Cromford & High Peak branch locomotive. **P**

For more information visit www.peakrail.co.uk

Royal Pioneer Corps was a British Army combatant corps used for light engineering tasks. It was formed in 1939 and amalgamated into the Royal Logistic Corps in 1993. Pioneer units performed a wide variety of tasks in all theatres of war, including stretcher-bearing, handling all types of stores, laying prefabricated track on beaches, and effecting various logistical operations. Under Royal Engineers supervision they constructed airfields and roads and erected bridges; they constructed the Mulberry Harbour and laid the Pipe Line Under the Ocean (PLUTO). See also *Sapper*.

For more information visit www.royalpioneercorps.co.uk/rpc/history_main1.htm

Pioneer Corps cap badge.

Preserved Austerity 0-6-0ST 'WD' No 75186/150 ROYAL PIONEER is seen as BR No 68013 at Peak Rail on 15 September 2012. *Rob Bendall*

MOS 'WD' Austerity 0-6-0 Saddle Tank, 1944 Robert Stephenson & Hawthorn built works number 7170, 'WD' No 71516 **WELSH GUARDSMAN**. This locomotive also saw service with the National Coal Board at Cynheidre Colliery. In 2016/17 this locomotive was reported as being operational at the site of the Gwili Railway. **P**

Welsh Guards Crest. *Gareth Wyn Jones*

For more information visit www.gwili-railway.co.uk/

 https://www.youtube.com/watch?v=ss2nSb0VrQ0
Gwili Railway, August 2014.

Welsh Guardsman. The Welsh Guards (WG), (*Gwarchodlu Cymreig*), part of the Guards Division, is one of the Foot Guards regiments of the British Army. It was founded on 26 February 1915 by Royal Warrant of King George V. The regiment served with distinction in both World Wars and was strengthened to three battalions during WWII. Post war the regiment has served in many regions of conflict including Suez, Northern Ireland, Bosnia, Falkland Islands, Iraq and Afghanistan. The famous regiment is still part of the British Army.

For more information visit www.army.mod.uk/infantry/regiments/23991.aspx

Preserved Austerity 0-6-0ST 'WD' No 71516 WELSH GUARDSMAN is seen at the Gwili Railway during the summer of 2014. *Keith Langston Collection*

For more information visit www.lakesiderailway.co.uk/

Repulse. HMS *Repulse* was a 'Renown' class battlecruiser built for the Royal Navy by John Brown & Co, Clydebank. The vessel was launched in January 1916 and commissioned in the August of that year, '*Repulse*' and her sister ship 'HMS *Renown*' were said to be the world's fastest 'capital ships' upon completion. The battlecruiser saw service in both World Wars and was sunk by a Japanese air attack off Kuantan, South China Sea on 10 December 1941. The destroyers HMS *Electra* and HMAS *Vampire* were quickly on hand and rescued many survivors, but sadly 508 crew members lost their lives.

Preserved Riddles/Hunslet design Austerity 0-6-0ST REPULSE (Hunslet built ex NCB locomotive) is seen at the Lakeside & Haverthwaite Railway in the summer of 2008. Note that the locomotive is fitted with a Giesl ejector for an explanation of that feature see SR Battle of Britain class section loco No 34064. *Len Mills*

For more information visit www.embsayboltonabbeyrailway.org.uk/

HMS *Warspite.* Seven ships of the Royal Navy have been named Warspite. The first recorded vessel being a 29-gun galleon launched in 1596. Of special note is HMS *Warspite* a Queen Elizabeth-class battleship launched in 1913. She served in the First World War and in numerous operations in the Second World War, earning the most battle honours of any Royal Navy ship. She ran aground on her way to be broken up in 1947 and was scrapped in 1950. The last British naval vessel to carry the name was a Valiant-class nuclear-powered submarine launched in 1965 and decommissioned in 1991.

'WD' Austerity design 0-6-0 Saddle Tank, 1953 Hunslet Engineering Co built works number 3791 K&ESR No 23 **HOLMAN F STEPHENS**. This locomotive was formerly 'WD' No 191 **BLACK KNIGHT** and was withdrawn by the army in August 1968. After being sold out of army service the engine arrived at the Kent & East Sussex Railway in February 1972. In 2017 this locomotive was reported as being operational at the K&ESR. **P**

0-6-0ST HOLMAN F STEPHENS at the Kent & East Sussex Railway.
Len Mills

Colonel Holman Fred Stephens (30 October 1868–23 October 1931) was a British light railway civil engineer and manager. He was engaged in engineering and building, and later managing, 16 light railways in England and Wales. His first commission was with the 1st Sussex (Volunteer) Royal Engineers as second-lieutenant in 1896. He was promoted to lieutenant in 1897 and in the following year to captain. He recruited 600 men to serve with the Royal Engineers in South Africa during the Boer War (1899-1902). With the rank of major, he became commanding officer of five companies of Royal Engineers in Kent. At the beginning of WW1 his companies were employed in the defence of the Thames and Medway estuaries, including responsibility for searchlights. In April 1916, he was transferred to the Territorial Force Reserve so that he could concentrate on managing his railways. In 1916 Stephens attained the rank of lieutenant-colonel in the Territorial

Army (TA) with which he had been associated since the 1890s. A museum devoted to his life and achievements is located at Tenterden Station in Kent. For more information visit www.hfstephens-museum.org.uk/holman-fred-stephens also www.youtube.com/watch?v=na5IE60eOtY

'WD' Austerity design 0-6-0 Saddle Tank, 1953 Hunslet Engineering Co built works number 3792. This locomotive was originally War Department No 192, and later No 92 named **WAGGONER**. In 2005 this locomotive was moved 'on loan' from the Army Museum to the Isle of Wight Steam Railway (IOWSR) with ownership being transferred to the IOWSR in 2008. In 2017 the locomotive was reported as being in service.

For more information visit www.iwsteamrailway.co.uk/locomotives.aspx

Waggoner. In military parlance, the name has long been associated with the Royal Logistic Corps (RLC) formerly the Royal Corps of Transport (RCT). The RLC comprises both Regular and Army Reserve units, it is the only (Combat Service Support) Corps of the British Army with battle honours. 'The Waggoner' publication is the journal of the Royal Corps of Transport, Royal Army Service Corps and Royal Corps of Transport Association. For more information visit http://trove.nla.gov.au/version/22253116

'WD' 0-6-0ST No 92 is seen at the Isle of Wight Steam Railway. *Len Mills*

'WD' Austerity design 0-6-0 Saddle Tank, 1953 Hunslet Engineering Co built works number 3796. This locomotive was originally War Department No 196 named **ERROL LONSDALE**. Whilst at the Longmoor Military Railway (LMR) the locomotive featured in the 1966 film The Great St. Trinians Train Robbery. After army service WD No 196 moved to the Mid Hants Railway in 1977 and then to the South Devon Railway in 1992. It was bought by an unnamed private buyer in 2009. In 2017 it was listed as operational at the Stoomcentrum Maldegem, a heritage railway located in Maldegem northern Belgium. In 2016 it was fully restored and given WD livery in 2016.

For more information visit http://www.stoomcentrum.be/en/

Major-General Errol Lonsdale, CB, MBE. Born 26/02/1913 in County Durham and died 03/03/2003 in Somerset. Lonsdale took a university direct commission into the Royal Army Service Corps (RASC) in 1934. He became Transport Officer-in-Chief [Army], 1966–69, Colonel-Commandant of the Royal Corps of Transport, 1969–74, and later ADC to Queen Elizabeth II. A committed railway enthusiast the Major General 'christened' the locomotive carrying his name in a ceremony held at the Longmoor Military Railway (LMR) in 1968.

Royal Corps of Transport wire badge. *Keith Langston Collection*

Shortly after refurbishment the smartly turned-out 'WD' No 196 is seen in action at the Stoomcentrum Maldegem in November 2016. *WDRB-RT*

'WD' Austerity design 0-6-0 Saddle Tank, 1953 Hunslet Engineering Co built works number 3798. This locomotive was originally War Department No 198, and was named **ROYAL ENGINEER** by them in 1971. In 1991 this locomotive was retired from service as the last working steam locomotive owned by the British Army. The locomotive was acquired for the Royal Corps of Transport Museum Trust at Chatham. As an interim measure, **ROYAL ENGINEER** was placed on loan to the Isle of Wight Steam Railway and, following the fitting of Westinghouse air brake equipment, was put to work on passenger services. In 2017 the locomotive was reported as being out of service awaiting boiler repairs. **P**

The Corps of Royal Engineers, usually simply referred to as the Royal Engineers (RE), and commonly known as the Sappers, is one of the corps of the British Army. It is highly regarded throughout the military, and especially the Army. It provides military engineering and other technical support to the British Armed Forces and is headed by the Chief Royal Engineer. The Regimental Headquarters and the Royal School of Military Engineering are in Chatham, Kent. The corps is divided into several regiments, which are barracked at various places in the United Kingdom and also around the world. The Royal Engineers trace their origins back to the military engineers brought to England by William the Conqueror, specifically Bishop Gundulf of Rochester Cathedral fame, and claim over 900 years of unbroken service to the British crown. Engineers have always served in the armies of the Crown; however, the origins of the modern corps, along with those of the Royal Artillery, lie in the Board of Ordnance established in the 15th century.

'WD' No 198 is seen after taking water at Havenstreet station on the route of the Isle of Wight Steam Railway. The railway runs just a little over five miles from Smallbrook Junction through Ashey and Havenstreet to Wootton. Note the Royal Corps of Transport crest on the locomotive's cabside. *David Jones*

'WD' Austerity design 0-6-0 Saddle Tank, 1954 Hunslet Engineering Co built works number 3823. Delivered new to the National Coal Board. Now named **WARRIOR** this locomotive is based at the Dean Forrest Railway (DFR). In 2017 the locomotive was reported as being under overhaul. **P**

For more information visit www.deanforestrailway.co.uk/

Warrior. In general, a professional soldier and/or person engaged in military life. Specifically, a soldier who has achieved distinction.

'WD' Austerity design 0-6-0 Saddle Tank, 1953 Hunslet Engineering Co built works number 3797. Delivered new to the War Department, WD No 197 **SAPPER**. Preserved at the K&ESR since 1977 as No 25 and re-named **NORTHIAM**. In 2017 the locomotive was reported as being stored out of use. **P**

Sapper. See earlier entry for Avon Valley Railway WD locomotive.

'WD' Austerity design 0-6-0 Saddle Tank, 1958 Hunslet Engineering Co built works number 3850. Ex ironstone Quarry Railways locomotive. Transferred to the IOWSR by the Ivatt Steam Trust in 2009 and named **JUNO**. Loaned to the NRM from October 2010 for display at Shildon. **P**

Crest of the Canadian armed forces.
Marco Kaiser

Juno or *Juno Beach.* One of five beaches of the Allied invasion of German occupied France in the Normandy landings on 6 June 1944, during the Second World War. The beach spanned from Courseulles, a village just east of the British beach Gold, to Saint-Aubin-sur-Mer, just west of the British beach Sword.

Taking Juno was the responsibility of the Canadian Army, with support provided by the Royal Canadian Navy and the Royal Navy and elements from the Free French, Norwegian, and other Allied navies.
The objectives of the 3rd Canadian Infantry Division on D-Day were to cut the Caen-Bayeux road, seize an airport to the west of Caen, and form a link between the two British beaches of Gold and Sword on either side of Juno Beach. The beach was defended by two battalions of the German 716th Infantry Division, with elements of the 21st Panzer Division held in reserve near Caen.

Class Details

| 'WD' Austerity Riddles/Hunslet Class Saddle Tank Locomotives

Also

BR 'J94' class

4F Classification | 0-6-0ST | 485 locomotives built by Hunslet Engine Company, Andrew Barclay Sons & Co, W.G. Bagnall, Hudswell Clarke, Robert Stephenson & Hawthorns and the Vulcan Foundry between 1943 and 1964. | Driving Wheel 4ft 3ins dia. | 2 – cylinders Stephenson slide valves | Working BP 170psi Superheated Tractive effort 23870 flb. Tractive effort 34,215 flb

Some slightly more powerful engines with 4ft diameter wheels were built between 1950 and 1953. Also with boiler pressure increased to 180psi. |

Andrew Barclay 0-4-0 Saddle Tank

Andrew Barclay 0-4-0 Saddle Tank, built at the Kilmarnock works and dating from 1914, works number 1385. Delivered to the Admiralty Royal Dockyard, Pembroke. Preserved circa February 1972. Reported as serviceable at the Chasewater Light Railway in 2017. **P**

For more information visit www.chasewaterrailway.co.uk/

Rosyth Dockyard. Rosyth Dockyard is a large naval dockyard on the Firth of Forth at Rosyth, Fife, Scotland, owned by Babcock Marine, which formerly undertook refitting of Royal Navy surface vessels and submarines. Before its privatisation in the 1990s it was formally the Royal Naval Dockyard Rosyth.

The name carried on brass plates by the Andrew Barclay 0-6-0ST in no way relates to the working history of the outside cylinder shunting locomotive. Without a doubt the Admiralty's intention was to employ the locomotive within the Rosyth Dockyard, Fife. However, the Admiralty needs at the Royal Dockyard, Pembroke, South Wales must have been considered greater as that is where this Barclay product first gained employment. The Royal Dockyard closed in 1926 but Rosyth No.1 remained on site in the ownership of the Air Ministry, who took over part of the Dockyard in 1930. Rosyth No.1 remained at Pembroke until displaced in 1955, it was then transferred to the Air Ministry, St. Athan, South Glamorgan. This was to be home for Rosyth No.1 for a further 18 years, and the Barclay saddle tank worked the traffic in sidings adjacent to the former Barry Railway's Barry to Bridgend line, a quarter mile north west of St. Athan station. The sidings were taken out of use on 7 May 1973.

Rosyth No.1's owners in preservation are the *Railway Club of Wales* (*Y Clwb Rheil Cymru*), who initially stored the loco for a short period at Morriston, and then the Swansea Industrial and Maritime Museum before transferring the locomotive to the Gwili Railway on 18 June 1987.

Recently, Rosyth No.1 has been based at the Pontypool and Blaenavon Railway and then on loan to the Chasewater Railway, having arrived there in July 2016. Steamings at Chasewater will reportedly be the locomotives first outside Wales.

USATC 'S160' 2-8-0 class

The United States Army Transportation Corps (USATC) 'S160' class of 2-8-0 locomotives were designed for wartime use in Europe on heavy freight work. As WWII progressed, and for a period thereafter the USA Austerity 2-8-0s also found use on many railways throughout the world and in total 2,120 examples were built. They were designed by Major J. W. Marsh U.S. Army, Railway Branch of the Corps of Engineers and built between 1942 and 1946. The builders were American Locomotive Co (ALCO) 755 locomotives, Baldwyn Locomotive Works 712 locomotives and Lima Locomotive Works 653 locomotives.

A total of 800 S160 locomotives were shipped to Great Britain. After landing in South Wales approximately 400 were prepared at GWR Newport depot and then transferred in varying quantities to the 'Big Four' railway companies GWR, LNER, LMSR and SR. A further total of 400 locomotives were prepared for storage by USATC personnel working at GWR Ebbw Junction depot, in the immediate run up to D-Day. As the Allied invasion of occupied Europe got underway almost all of the S160 locomotives working in Britain were, over a short period of time, taken out of service and moved to Ebbw Junction in preparation for shipment to Europe.

The aforementioned first batch of 400 S160 class locomotives were allocated to the British railway companies under the guise of 'running in' but in fact were put to work replacing damaged and out of service engines in addition to complementing others in order to cope with the increase in pre-D-day rail movements. Regional S160 locomotive allocation totals for the period were as follows: – 174 to the Great Western Railway (GWR)
168 to the London & North Eastern Railway (LNER)
50 to the London, Midland & Scottish Railway (LMSR) 6 to the Southern Railway (SR)

Which totalled 398 locomotives, it is likely that the remaining 2 engines were sent to the Longmoor Military Railway (LMR) for evaluation. Given the frequency of attacks on Atlantic convoys by enemy U-Boats etc., it is remarkable that no S160 locomotives were reportedly lost during the many supply voyages to Britain. For more information visit www.lner. info/locos/O/s160.php

www.youtube.com/watch?v=ahGJPutGs4A

USATC S160 2-8-0 LMR No 700 MAJOR-GEN CARL R. GRAY JR is seen at Longmoor Downs during a public day in 1955. *Mike Morant Collection*

USATC 2-8-0 S160, LMR No 93257 **MAJOR GENERAL CARL R. GRAY JNR** built by American Locomotive Co in 1944, Works No 71512. This locomotive operated at the Longmoor Military Railway during WWII and was listed in the LMR 1949 stock list. Scrapped circa 1957.

Brigadier General Carl R. Gray Jr. (14 April 1889–2 December 1955), was the chief executive of a railroad company in the western USA and a veteran of World War 1. Prior to WWII he held a reserve commission as a Colonel. When the USA entered WWII Gray was called to active service as Manager Military Railway Service. He became a Major General and then went on to become Director of Allied Railway Services. Major General Carl R. Gray Jr., originally from Wichita, Kansas, and later Hudson, Wisconsin, claimed to have moved 42 times in his first 50 years. During World War II, Gray was in overall command of the Military Railway Service for the United States Army in both the European and African theatres from 1943 until 1945.

Preservation

There are at least 26 preserved S160 class locomotives world wide and 6 of them are located in the UK, all of which have been imported from other countries, although some did serve in the UK during World War II. The UK railway centres which list S160 examples as part of their fleet are the Keighley & Worth Valley Railway (K&WVR), the Churnet Valley Railway (CVR), the Birmingham Railway Museum, the North Yorkshire Moors Railway (NYMR), the Great Central Railway (Nottingham) and the Mid Hants Railway (MHR). The MHR example carries the name FRANKLIN D. ROOSEVELT.

USATC 2-8-0 S160, No 3278 **FRANKLIN D. ROOSEVELT** built by Baldwyn Locomotive Works in 1944, Works No 70340. This locomotive was imported from Greece in 1984 where it ran as No FS 736.073 and was reportedly under repair at Tyseley Locomotive Works in 2017.

Born on 30 January 1882, in Hyde Park, New York, Franklin Delano Roosevelt was stricken with polio in 1921. He became the 32nd U.S. president in 1933, and was the only president to be elected four times. Roosevelt led the United States through the Great Depression and World War II, and died in Georgia in 1945. FDR is rightly remembered as a great wartime leader. He sought ways to assist China in its war with Japan and declared that France and Great Britain were America's 'first line of defence' against Nazi Germany. In 1940, Roosevelt began a series of measures to help defend France and Britain, including the Lend-Lease agreement. For more information visit www.biography.com/people/franklin-d-roosevelt-9463381#us-presidency

*Lend-Lease. The Lend-Lease policy, formally titled 'An Act to Promote the Defense of the United States', enacted 11 March 1941, was a programme under which the United States supplied Free France, the United Kingdom, the Republic of China, the Soviet Union and other Allied nations with food, oil, and materials between 1941 and August 1945. This included warships, warplanes, and weaponry, and included railway equipment. Lend-Lease ended in September 1945. In general, the aid was free, although some hardware (such as ships) were returned after the war. Where appropriate the U.S. was given leases on army and naval bases in Allied territory during the war in return. In the monetary value of the period Lend-Lease aid supplied to the British Empire was estimated to have exceeded $31 million.

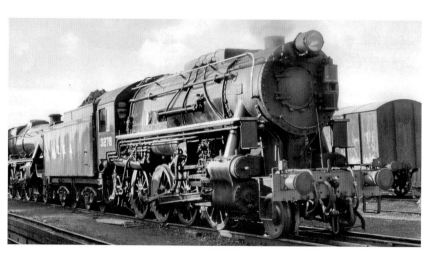

USATC 2-8-0 S160, No 3278 FRANKLIN D. ROOSEVELT is seen at the Mid- Hants Railway. *Keith Langston Collection*

The photographing of the country's railways and railway equipment during the war time period was forbidden hence the fact that very few images of S160 locomotives at work on the national network exist. Consequently, this image of US Transportation Corps 2-8-0 No 2454 taken 'somewhere in the British Midlands' was in all probability created after V-E Day (Victory in Europe 8 May 1945). Note the splendid lattice signal post and bracket. *Rail Photoprints Collection*

Class Details

'USATC S160' Austerity Locomotives	2-8-0	Total built 2,120 locomotives American Locomotive Co (ALCO) 755 Baldwyn Locomotive Works 712 Lima Locomotive Works 653	Driving Wheel 4ft 9ins dia.	2 – cylinders Walschaert piston valves	Working BP 225psi Superheated Tractive effort 31,490flb

USATC 'S100' class 0-6-0T

The United States Army Transportation Corps (USATC) S100 Class is a 0-6-0T steam locomotive that was designed for switching (shunting) duties in Europe and North Africa during World War II. Several were later used on railways in Austria, Great Britain, France, Greece, Italy, Yugoslavia, Palestine, Iraq, Iran, Israel and China. The S100 is a side tank design by Col. Howard G. Hill. In 1942, the USATC ordered a total of 382 S100s from the Davenport Locomotive Works of Iowa, H. K. Porter, Inc, of Pittsburgh and Vulcan Iron Works of Wilkes-Barre. They were shipped to Great Britain in 1943 where they were stored until 1944. After D-Day, they were shipped to Continental Europe. British Railways took into stock 14 operational examples and they were allocated to the Southern Region, running numbers 30061–30074. In 1962/3 6 of the class were transferred to the SR Service Locomotives list as D233–D238. One example operated at the LMR. There are 6 preserved examples in the UK of which 4 are ex BR and 2 are imports from the former Yugoslavia. In 2017 one of the class, BR No 30065 was reported as being operational at the Kent & East Sussex Railway (K&ESR). For more information visit http://www.kesr.org.uk/

> USATC S100 0-6-0T, LMR No 94382 MAJOR GENERAL FRANK S. ROSS built by Davenport in 1943, Works No 2531. This locomotive operated at the Longmoor Military Railway during WWII and was listed in the LMR 1949 stock list.

As the USA entered WWII it was soon realised that Great Britain, being only 35 miles from mainland Europe was the obvious place from which to launch an invasion of Nazi held European countries. The subsequent plan to base a large military force in Britain brought with it logistical challenges, e.g. by the end of June 1942 56,090 US troops and their equipment were based in the country. To that end the issue of transportation was addressed when the War Department in conjunction with US Army Forces British Isles (USAFBI) assigned Col. (later Maj. Gen.) Frank S. Ross as Chief of Transportation for USAFBI.

'USA 0-6-0T S100' class (Davenport 2531/1943) FRANK S. ROSS on shed at the Longmoor Military Railway, on 3 September 1955. *Hugh Ballantyne/Rail Photoprints*

Class Details

'USATC S100' Austerity Locomotives	0-6-0T	Total 382 built Davenport Locomotive Works 109 H K Porter Inc 150 Vulcan Iron Works 123	Driving Wheel 4ft 6ins dia	2 – cylinders Walschaert piston valves	Working BP 210psi Tractive effort 21,630flb

Military Connections – LMS & LNER Locomotives

by the same author and also published by *Pen & Sword Books* is the perfect companion for this volume, due to release in late 2018.

For Keith Langston's other Transport titles also in print with Pen & Sword, please see the following link:
https://www.pen-and-sword.co.uk/Keith-Langston/a/1802

Rail Photoprints

For the best in editorial photo files and images of Steam and Modern Traction, in the UK and further afield.

http://railphotoprints.uk/